IT Quality Management

Wolfgang W. Osterhage

IT Quality Management

 Springer

Wolfgang W. Osterhage
Wachtberg-Niederbachem,
Germany

Translation from the German language edition: Abnahme komplexer Softwaresysteme. Das Praxishandbuch. (©) Springer-Verlag Berlin Heidelberg 2009

ISBN 978-3-662-51553-2   ISBN 978-3-662-43767-4 (eBook)
DOI 10.1007/978-3-662-43767-4
Springer Heidelberg New York Dordrecht London

Springer is part of Springer Science+Business Media (www.springer.com)

Contents

Chapter 1
Objectives

1.1 Introduction

This book has grown from practice and is intended to serve practitioners. It has been built upon nearly 20 years of experience in tests, acceptance and certification, when implementing medium to large IT systems including complex software in industry and other organisations in many countries. As is well known there exist different methodologies with different characteristics having emanated from various schools and consultancies to support such activities. However, it is obvious that—depending on the organisational levels in companies—the rigor of application of such methodologies suffers to the benefit of more pragmatic approaches. In view of economic objectives this quite often is unavoidable. For this reason no new or consolidated methodology shall be presented here but an approach oriented on practical criteria coming close to reality and offering methods, which can provide assistance on an individual basis.

After discussing objectives and the limits of this book the subject itself will be entered by outlining possible project organisations, which are suited for such complex tasks. Within an overall organisation IT quality management is part of it. The focus here is on processes in the context of software acceptance. Against this backdrop IT quality management can be divided into separate sub-responsibilities.

Furthermore the basics of acceptance procedures will be outlined resulting in an example for an acceptance directive or policy, which may serve as a template, agreed upon both by customers and software providers.

Because quite often data migration is part of the introduction of new systems, it will be discussed in a separate chapter. Other special considerations regard acceptance of interfaces, customising, building of test clients and performance. Eventually the subject of documentation will be touched upon within the framework of software delivery. Finally short presentations of classical tools for project management and IT project controlling will round up the book.

© Springer-Verlag Berlin Heidelberg 2014
W.W. Osterhage, *IT Quality Management*, DOI 10.1007/978-3-662-43767-4_1

Each chapter with the exception of this introduction and the appendices are structured in a similar way:

- Introduction
- Problem area
- Organisational solution
- Instruments
- Templates
- Summary of approach.

1.2   Scope

The scope of this book and some of its guidelines are characterised by two limitations:

- System relevance and
- Time relevance.

System relevance refers to the complexity and the level of change with regard to software. Obviously the proposed methods can be applied to any kind of software. For economical reasons, however, they are less relevant for small and standard applications.

The time scope normally refers to states of document versions such as an acceptance directive or some of the documents discussed in Chap. 8. Each document is identified by a version ID referring to the main document. Its validity is based on the current version, only exceptionally on sections of predecessor versions. In any case the latest update of a document normally is the valid one. All changes to any document have to be recorded as a version history until final clearance.

1.3   Methodologies

The implementation of complex systems will normally be achieved by setting up a proper project of its own or by using the structure of an already existing project. There are now a number of methodologies, which can be employed to facilitate the acceptance procedures. To those belong for example CMMI (Capability Maturity Model Integration), SPICE (Software Process and Capability Determination) and ITIL. CMMI helps to judge and improve the quality for product development processes. This means it precedes proper quality control itself from the perspective of customers, but also covers initial sections of the overall process chain such as request management for example. SPICE is a true norm (ISO/IEC 15504), which initially validates enterprise processes in general, but emphasizes software

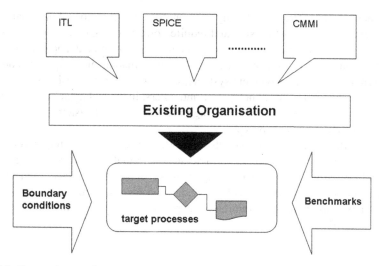

Fig. 1.1 Pragmatic procedures

development. Parts of it deal with customer-supplier-processes. The ITIL library has grown into a work of reference and thus into a near standard and covers among many other things also such processes as release and change management. All these cited norms and other methodologies will not be discussed in detail here.

However, from those meanwhile classical methodologies like ITIL or SPICE quite often only fragments are used in practise. The reasons for this are to be found in grown structures and processes in companies. A comprehensive and complete mapping for example of the business environment according to ITIL standards prior to project start is often difficult because of associated costs and time pressure. This book delivers a neutral approach, which has been put to many tests in practise. This does not exclude that occasionally some elements from one or the other book of rules may appear as well. In the end there is only a limited spectrum of possible approaches for identical problem scenarios. Figure 1.1 shows schematically the relationships between standard methodologies and the approach offered in this book.

1.4 Complex Systems

Generally speaking, complex systems normally surpass an individual standard product, which means that they include cross linking between different systems, each of which has to take care of its proper tasks in the business environment in a company. The functioning of such cross linking has to take place via special interfaces. Furthermore complex systems quite often contain software components, which have to be tailored or developed from scratch with regard to specific requirements of organisations. In any case one has to take into account that such systems are subject to customising and require corresponding parameterization.

Such systems for example are large business and technical applications. To quote but some, they comprise ERP, CRM, store management, quality control systems, maintenance management systems, support systems for business processes in utilities, billing in telecommunications and others. In the technical field there are: CAD, finite element calculation and design methods, control systems, simulations and model calculations in physics.

It is important that there is a significant portion of customising required on the one hand (including development from scratch) and that there is some degree of complexity regarding functional variety, number of users, interface connections and data volumes. In case applications under consideration do not or only rudimentary meet these boundary conditions the proposed methods in this book will be difficult to justify for economic reasons.

Chapter 2
Project Organisation

2.1 Quality Management as a Project

To start with one has to differentiate between the line function "IT Quality Management" and some quality management project. Acceptance of new software or new releases or parts of it typically fulfils project characteristics:

- Defined starting point
- Defined end point
- Clearly stated terms of reference
- Participation of specially requested specialists from different departments.

Furthermore there exists the possibility that the sub-project "acceptance" can be part of a wider project context such as re-structuring efforts. The management of such a project or sub-project will be carried out by the organisational unit "IT Quality Management", if a company has one. Otherwise a temporary structure has to be created for such a project. If a similar project exists, under certain circumstances its structures and resources may be used.

The following explications assume that the development unit of the software vendor has its own proper quality management. His quality management takes care that only quality assured software components are delivered to the customer. This means:

- Tested by developers and
- Clearly versionised modules ordered by the customer.

Correspondingly the customer creates capabilities to verify that "delivery takes place of what had been ordered". Just as with any other goods entry, order and delivery are balanced against each other and possible discrepancies recorded for later correction. Reference basis for the order are functional specifications mutually agreed upon beforehand. While the internal quality management of the supplier carries out some sort of "factory acceptance" for his concerns the customer quality

© Springer-Verlag Berlin Heidelberg 2014
W.W. Osterhage, *IT Quality Management*, DOI 10.1007/978-3-662-43767-4_2

management approves the delivered software with the aim to put it into quality approved operation after acceptance procedures.

Quality management of the customer thus not only fulfils its original core business mission but in the end also clears the supplier's bill for payment by the customer. Thus it provides a strategic function in the context of an implementation project. Therefore it has to be assigned a corresponding role of importance in an organisation and in the context of a given project.

2.2   Overall Process

The management of an implementation project, in which decision makers of the supplier as well as those from the customer take part, makes sure that the whole chain of processes between original request until error and data clean-up—until even after the start date of operations—is worked through in time and that agreed upon quality criteria are respected. For that matter it is of no importance whether this refers to a complete release or to for example only the implementation of change requests. Identical procedures apply.

The following steps are part of this overall process (Fig. 2.1):

- Request management
- Change management
- Error management
- Quality management

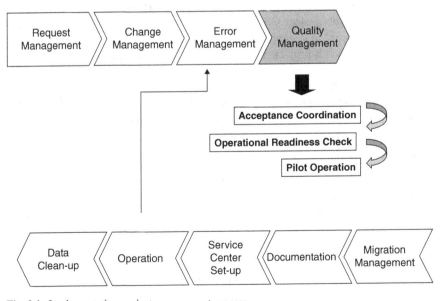

Fig. 2.1 Implementation project management process

- Migration management
- Documentation
- Operations
- Data clean-up

Quality management comprises:

- Acceptance coordination
- Operational readiness check
- Trial operation.

Normally the functional segments depicted sequentially in Fig. 2.1 are carried out overlapping or phase shifted. The sequence in the diagram only underlines their logical interdependence. Different tasks are naturally taken care of in different approaches corresponding to the acceptance object. A single change request to be implemented will require less attention than a complete release from the planning phase to operational readiness.

2.3 Sub-project Structures

Depending on the importance of the tasks outlined above responsibilities in an implementation project are distributed in such a way that they form a sub-project structure (Fig. 2.2).

In this figure the tasks

- Request management
- Change management
- Error management

are grouped together with overall release planning. This need not always be the case. Error management could for example be a sub-project in its own right.

Quality management comprises the responsibilities outlined in Fig. 2.1. A separation of one of them into a different sub-project would not make sense.

Some problem areas related to data management or data quality etc. are grouped together under a single sub-project responsibility.

Operations, service centre and documentation have not been separated as individual sub-projects. They can be assigned to one of the three fields of competence— for example documentation as part of quality management—or temporarily integrated from line functions into a project (service centre and operations). Interface operations are mentioned explicitly here. The reason for this is that there is quite often the requirement to run certain interfaces independently from end user intervention via separate job control scripts by a service centre.

The processes and responsibilities depicted in Figs. 2.1 and 2.2 present only an extract from the overall process world. Development, project planning and controlling and other functions have been left out on purpose, since only functions in

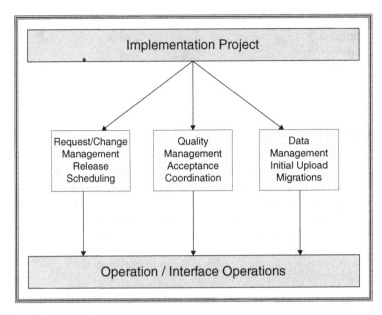

Fig. 2.2 Project organisation

connection with quality are to be regarded here. These will be discussed in detail following the sequence of their logical linkage.

2.3.1 Request Management

If possible, request management should consolidate all requests for one and the same implementation project into one single software package to be realised or enhanced. These requests can originate from different sources:

- Description of the overall scope of a package: this can be the result of workshops or a complete documentation of all relevant business processes in a company.
- Demands from the user community for new functions
- Demands from the user community concerning specific functional enhancements
- Lessons learned and proposals from the supplier of the system to better assist work flows
- Technical requirements resulting from user experience with existing software.

Request management collects all these demands. They can be posted sporadically or be based on workshop consultations to prepare for a major update or a completely new release. It has proven useful to consolidate and structure all demands into a data base with status tracking, such as:

- Open
- Ordered
- In realisation
- Accepted
- In operation.

Before specific requests can be dealt with, they should be formulated as functional specifications. A standard structure for this should be employed. Cost estimates can be formulated only after agreement with the supplier on these specifications. The eventual order for realisation depends of course also on priorities and budget available.

After ordering the supplier can then draft his technical specifications. As functional specifications are concerned with the business content itself, technical specifications describe, how realisation will proceed. Therefore we have two more status items for requests:

- Functional specifications drafted and accepted
- Technical specifications drafted and accepted.

Agreement to those documents should be granted by representatives from the business units of the customer.

To ease later acceptance procedures, which will follow realisation, different requests should be collected and grouped together as releases or versions with fixed milestones, presenting the time basis for acceptance. Sometimes this is difficult to sustain throughout the proceedings. Because of priorities resulting from technical or functional urgencies or from influences from outside the project there is always the possibility to deliver special functional packages in between. Normally, however, request management in cooperation with the supplier should produce a binding release schedule with milestone end dates.

To track the actual status of specific requests agreed communication and feedback procedures between request management and all parties concerned are necessary, including:

- User/requester
- Development unit of the supplier
- Quality management/acceptance coordination
- Operations support.

2.3.1.1 Tender Procedures

Request management together with purchasing, IT managers and business units should participate in tender procedures for new software. We will not look at the commercial selection process here. It is important that pricing and agreement about delivery dates should be based on documents agreed upon by all parties. These documents are the functional and technical specifications mentioned above.

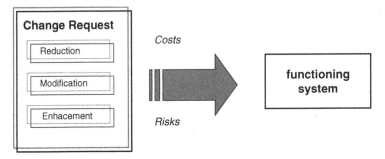

Fig. 2.3 Change management

2.3.2   Change Management

Quite often change management is part of request management proper, since it uses similar processes (Fig. 2.3).

Experience with software in operation quite often leads to change requests, regularly as individual user requests demanding changes to existing functions. Sometimes this means reducing the scope of existing functions because business has changed for example. Sometimes they ask for modifications because processes have changed. Initiators of such change requests come from

- The user community
- The development unit of the supplier.

Before such requests are placed in the request management data base for tracking, a careful cost-risk evaluation should take place, where risk relates to technical and business factors, but also budgetary risks have to be taken into account. Beyond dispute are all requests necessary for the correct functioning of business processes including the technical functioning of the system. Not always all functional consequences are reflected in advance during the phase of functional specifications, and process inconsistencies become apparent only after intensive use of the realised product.

Treatment of change requests follows along identical lines as ordinary requests within the scope of request management. Because of different priorities realisation and putting into operation may sometimes happen between long term scheduled release milestones.

2.3.3   Error Management

Software errors are detected and reported in different instances:

- During operation in daily business by end users
- During an enhancement project based on already existing functions
- During acceptance tests prior to putting software into operation, meaning in the course of quality management proper.

Initiators:

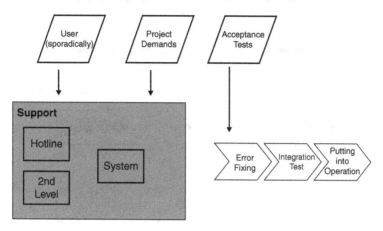

Fig. 2.4 Error management

Figure 2.4 shows the general procedure after error detection.

With the exception of errors detected during acceptance tests all other errors follow a support chain normally starting by activating a hotline to a call centre. Second level support intervenes only, when the hotline is not capable to render a useful contribution to resolve the error (in this case one has to take into account that quite often errors reported by end users are due to operating errors; in the following only real software errors will be discussed). Feedback from technical departments shall not be discussed here.

The treatment of errors from acceptance tests will be elaborated further down. This concerns deliveries of corrections during acceptance tests as well.

All corrections are carried out after error reports and corresponding corrections are tested on the basis of the same acceptance procedures—quite similar to realised change requests or other acceptance objects—sometimes in abbreviated fashion. Figure 2.5 details errors types and their corresponding handling processes.

Something subjectively appearing as an error may have different causes:

- Real software errors, having been created while converting technical specifications into code,
- Correctly realised requests, but leading to wrong business results during operation (algorithms, plausibility checks etc.),
- Data errors coming for example from data migration from other cross-linked systems; these can be of various origins and are not discussed any further here.

According to error type the correction process follows its own procedure:

- Error correction as mentioned above,
- As a change request to initiate a new functional amendment
- Passing on to a sub-project, which is responsible for data clean-up.

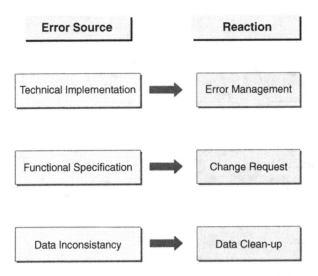

Fig. 2.5 Error sources

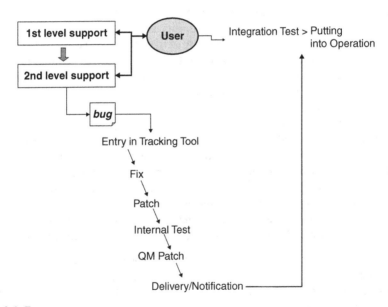

Fig. 2.6 Error process

2.3.3.1 Technical Error Management

When he finds a problem the user calls a service hotline (first level support) (Fig. 2.6):

In case the problem is classified as an error and this error cannot be resolved during the call the caller will be given a reference or ticket number. The hotline

Assessment Status	Work Status	Modul	Type	Reported by	Actual Owner	Description	Priority ID
open	entered	xyz	error	Jones	Brown	short text	2 #num

Fig. 2.7 Tracking tool

forwards the problem with an appropriate description to the second level support. After checking and reproducing the error it is entered into a tracking tool (Fig. 2.7).

The tracking tool is a software supported instrument to follow up error corrections. This tool should be based upon at least the following items:

- *Assessment status:* open, rejected, closed
- *In work status:* entered, in progress, finished, quality assured, delivered
- *Module:* identification of the relevant module of the software package
- *Type:* error, change request
- *Reported by:* name of the person, who first reported the problem (user)
- *Actual owner:* person, taking care of the problem at the moment
- *Description:* short text
- *Priority:* 1, 2, 3
- *ID:* numerical identification code.

Once the error has been entered in the tool it will be attended to within the work schedule of the development unit by taking its priority into account (priority "1") after consultation with the customer. Once the in work status reaches "finished" a first patch for internal testing is loaded onto the development system. If it passes successfully a quality assured patch is loaded onto the test system of the customer, the in work status changes to "quality assured" and the customer is notified for acceptance test.

Thereafter the usual acceptance procedures apply. After successful acceptance the new software is put into operation. The in work status changes to "delivered" and the assessment status to "closed".

2.4   Autonomy of Sub-projects

The sub-projects listed under Sect. 2.2 have to be in phase with each other and have certain formalities in common. However, it does not make much sense to control them centrally concerning every detail. Thus the principle of subsidiary should hold meaning that professional knowledge as well as responsibility should reside on the level of execution. It is quite sufficient that agreement is reached on the following subjects:

- Overall mile stone schedule
- Budget distributed across the individual sub-projects
- Responsibilities
- Reporting procedures.

It remains with the sub-projects to achieve their objectives in their own responsibility. For this responsible managers of the sub-projects employ those instruments, which they deem fit for their purposes. However, one has to make sure that communication proceeds along agreed upon lines. If necessary, this can be assured by drafting internal Service Level Agreements (SLAs). Of course the overall project is subject to a central controlling instance with special emphasis on budget control.

In large organisations most of the sub-project responsibilities remain intact even after the project has come to an end. They can be utilised for follow-up projects. In small companies tasks like migration and data clean-up will have finished with the end of such a project. They can be re-activated at a later stage, if required. However, there is a risk that acquired knowhow may have been lost by then once external resources have been released.

2.5   Templates

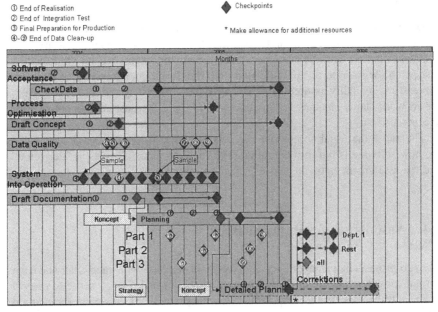

Fig. 2.8 Mile stone plan

Month1		Request	Req. No.	Budget
	Name1			
	Name2			
	Name3			
Month2	Name1			
	Name2			
	Name3			
....				
Monthx	Name1			
	Name2			
	Name3			
Sum	Name1			
	Name2			
	Name3			

Fig. 2.9 Budget plan

Project Status: Project Name   Date of Report:

Mile Stone	Degree of Completion	Problems	Measures
Designation Task1 Task2			
Designation Task1 Task2			
Designation Task1 Task2			
Designation Task1 Task2			

Fig. 2.10 Status report

2.6   Approach

Defining an acceptance undertaking as a project > making sure that all sub-projects of the business are taken into account > sub-projects running autonomously > implementation of common reporting procedures.

Chapter 3
Quality Management and Acceptance

3.1 Quality Management

Although the sub-processes discussed so far do not belong to the core business of quality management they are essential to it as front ends or as parts of feedback loops. In the overall project structure quality management represents a sub-project in its own right. It runs its proper reporting with interfaces to the main project. In the following we will discuss its:

- Scope
- Responsibilities and
- Detailed tasks.

3.2 Scope

In general the customer's quality management serves to assure a high quality of realised software components including interfaces, when implementing complex software systems, prior to putting them into operation. All industry standards available for this purpose and being partly or in total relevant have to be taken into consideration. But respecting ISO is not an objective in itself but is driven by the interests and economic considerations of all parties concerned. Therefore the overall objectives with respect to (elaborate) acceptance procedures can be formulated as follows:

3.2.1 Avoidance of Long Pilot Operations

How this works out practically will be discussed further down. Test objectives are oriented to reduce costs and effort and to eliminate bottlenecks (with respect to mile stones). Quite often software is developed under high time pressure. Reasons for

© Springer-Verlag Berlin Heidelberg 2014
W.W. Osterhage, *IT Quality Management*, DOI 10.1007/978-3-662-43767-4_3

this are to be found in the requirement to bring certain parts of the business to market early and competitively. From this mile stone backwards scheduling is undertaken to calculate the date of putting into operation and therefore in the end the start date of software development and other previous mile stone dates (functional specifications, technical specifications). Since development capacity is limited time pressure arises as a matter of course.

One possibility to gain more time is to avoid long pilot operations. Pilot operation in this context means the simulation of real operations on a test system, which mirrors the real world including its complete data base either before going into real operation or in parallel with it. Pilot operations until final clearance for going life do not only require calendar time but will bind development, quality and especially end user resources extensively.

It is quality management that can influence the optimisation of time and resources by taking care that nearly error free software can go into pilot operation in as much as the latter is still deemed necessary. Ideally the acceptance process itself should be sufficient making pilot operations completely superfluous.

3.2.2 Avoidance of Production Breakdown

With or without pilot operation the objective is to avert negative consequences after putting software into operation, which has not been tested sufficiently. This sounds quite obvious. But total system breakdown is not always necessary to let daily business grind to a halt. Inefficient control of screen sequences, systematic data errors from updates via interfaces or the failure of a critical algorithm suffice to block the work schedule of users. And exactly these kinds of errors or inefficiencies do not show up during development tests.

A careful selection of test beds as well as a thorough and comprehensive design of test scripts allows for a maximum number of variants for a business process to be tested. As elsewhere: the point is that the effort to be invested has to be exerted in any case. If it is not done at the early stages, costs will multiply later on.

3.2.3 Instant Resolution of Faults

The discussion regarding error handling shows clearly that error detection and amendment loops are most cost-efficient and controllable during acceptance tests by quality management. The identification as well as control of measures to be taken resulting from error detection during production at a later stage will generate significantly more communication overheads compared to error detection during acceptance tests by project specialists, who have participated in drafting the functional specifications. Furthermore these specialists quite often have direct access to the responsible developers. This facilitates rapid clarification.

The patch cycle agreed upon prior to acceptance tests is particularly helpful allowing practically immediate error resolution (with only minor temporary inconvenience for the test business) by hot fixes for example. This can be followed up directly by additional tests of the corrected versions.

Software corrections resulting from production problems at a later stage have to follow the scheduling of updates. A prompt implementation therefore is only possible in exceptional cases—for example in extreme breakdown situations—with all the risks for active production during uploading and later executing untested changes. When changes to the data model have to be done, longer downtimes are unavoidable.

3.2.4   Avoidance of Data Inconsistencies

When linking different systems, each of which cover specific parts of a business, and which exchange data and have access to the same data base, the problem of data consistency may arise. For systems having been designed from scratch this problem should be negligible or non-existing. However, it may become virulent once one or more existing systems are linked up, since every system including its associated data pool has its own history.

Later, when dealing with data migration (Chap. 6) preventive measures will be discussed. Indispensable, however, is a carefully prepared interface test, if possible with real life data, not only to ensure interface functioning but also to check data quality regarding consistency and rejection rates. Data clean-up projects to be initiated later for production data files, because previous testing had been neglected, are very costly and may take a long time. In most cases those measures will lag behind the ever changing actual data base constantly modified during production. It can be very costly with regard to data that are visible to the outside world like bills to customers for example.

To recapitulate:

> The economic aim of quality management during implementation for complex IT systems is the avoidance of heavy costs during later stages. Experience shows that omission of investments at the early project stage quite often results in later amendments, costing up to 200 % or more of preventive measures.

3.3   Responsibilities of Quality Management

Roughly speaking the main responsibility of quality management focuses on scheduling and managing acceptance tests prior to final delivery of software or interfaces to be put into operation. All other responsibilities result from input from other sub-processes or standard practise. The latter are caused by the interplay with activities either prior to acceptance tests or follow them up as consequences of test results (as lined out above and to be detailed further down). The overall task of quality management is facilitated by drafting generally agreed upon acceptance specifications as part of an implementation project.

As already indicated, quality management initially takes on the role of goods entry by applying the rules:

1. Ordered goods: technical specifications
2. Delivered goods: software.

Deviations are recorded as errors, before a final decision concerning possible rejection of the delivery or parts thereof is made.

The responsibilities of ordinary goods entry are exceeded in the sense that quality management also is responsible to follow up on possible subsequent deliveries in the form of amendments and corrections until the original delivery of all ordered software runs without faults.

The responsibilities in detail comprise the following:

- Identification of test requirements
- Define personal responsibilities within the framework of acceptance tests
- Overall scheduling of acceptance tests together with the supplier
- Managing acceptance tests
- Final validation and recommendation.

3.3.1   Identification of Test Requirements

According to acceptance of one of the objects

- Release
- Special functions/individual change requests
- Error amendments
- Data migration,

the requirements for acceptance tests may vary. To begin with, the following essential resources have to be considered:

- Hardware and system environment, and there again

  1. Server environment with the performance required for the tasks at hand,
  2. Configuration, including subsystems and utilities necessary for the software to be tested and to run without faulty configuration parameters,

3. Sufficient external storage space,
4. Number and type of terminals and their localisation, if necessary special provisions for remote access via networks,
5. Planning and preparation of the test locations required;

- Test personnel from end user departments to be cleared with department heads for the duration of the tests, specialists from the implementation project, who did participate in drafting the functional specifications, and support from the supplier—in most cases developers, who did part of the realisation;
- Allocation of functions to be tested to specialists capable of drafting the appropriate test scripts;
- Identification and ordering test data, including the fundamental decision, whether tests should be carried out with real or synthetic data;
- Provisions for interfaces, the input or output of which are essential to test important functions, if necessary including interface simulations with the help of log files.

All these resources listed above have to be taken into account by the acceptance coordination, which can be taken care of by a special sub-project management and by IT quality management at the same time, and scheduled in detail with a sufficient time buffer prior to acceptance test start taking target dates and responsible personnel resources into account.

3.3.2 Defining Personal Responsibilities for the Acceptance Process

After the general identification of personnel resources individual test tasks have to be attached to names (not organisational units!). Authors for functional specifications and co-authors for technical specifications together with the supplier have to be named, if these documents do not yet exist. However, for a professionally run project one can expect that those documents are available and cleared prior to the actual start of the acceptance tests.

Quite often the persons having been involved in the specifications are at the same time in charge of drafting the test scripts. At this instance representatives from the user environment should be drawn in. Parallel to drafting test scripts test data are to be defined. The authors of the test scripts will be those persons, who will in the end also carry out the acceptance tests in their specific professional field. They will be supported by the relevant business units. If not already done so, the management of the sub-project "Quality Management" now has to obtain an agreement from the responsible managers of the business units in question—if possible, in writing—concerning the release of testers for the test duration and location. This is all the more important for testing not being executed at the work place of the persons requested. This should be the preferred scenario to avoid distraction by daily business.

The supplier should be asked to provide development resources for the functionalities in question for the duration of the tests—at least in stand-by mode. Furthermore, the presence of the internal quality management of the supplier is essential in case amendment patches or hot fixes are to be introduced during acceptance testing.

System specialists covering different competences should be named and scheduled for the operation of the test environment.

If not already defined by the intrinsic structure of the implementation project itself, escalation paths and instances have to be defined and this for three reasons:

- To make decisions in case of conflict regarding classification of errors,
- To decide on the abandonment or continuation of acceptance procedures, if serious disruptions occur (system problems, software breakdown, bottlenecks regarding personnel resources etc.),
- To serve as addressee of the final acceptance report.

3.3.3 Coordination of Test Scripts and Test Data

Test scripts emanate from three sources:

- Functional specifications
- Technical specifications
- Business processes.

All three depend on each other. One should assume that functional specifications are always drafted on the basis of documented business processes. Those in turn serve as the basis for the technical specifications to be written by developers. This is the theory. Only, when these preconditions are met can test scripts finally be drafted on the sole basis of business processes. Unfortunately only in few companies comprehensive and up-to-date documented business processes are to be found. Regarding specific functions, that may have been developed, possibly driven even by ad-hoc insights during the usage of existing software, this is even less the case. Therefore one has to assume a rather heterogenic document history, when suddenly and under time pressure acceptance tests become urgent.

The supplier will always take the latest version of the technical specifications as a reference for his billing. From a legal point of view this is quite in order. However, the end user will give his approval only in case the new functions support his business processes in such a way as he deems appropriate. This last criterion has priority. To avoid conflict all parties concerned should be permanently consulted. If necessary, compromises have to be agreed upon, if differences arise in spite of all the communication during the drafting process of the specifications. Fact is: the software has arrived by now.

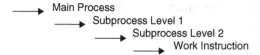

The level „Work Instruction" permits in turn variants by using the variables „Start Condition" and „Input".

The combination of the three items „Work Instruction", „Start Condition" and „Input" can be identified unequivocally with the help of a code number following the process hierarchy.

Acceptance Criteria

For each identifiable test case there exist acceptance criteria consisting of
- expected output and
- objective (with reference to the work instruction).

Fig. 3.1 Process hierarchy

In no case the customer should be satisfied by just accepting the test scripts from the development tests of the supplier, since those are oriented along purely technical criteria without any focus on the business processes themselves. In this context it is important to emphasise that testing has to be carried out on the level of work instructions. This level is depicted in Fig. 3.1.

Figure 3.1 presents a basic schema. With respect to the complexity of the main process the hierarchy can be more or less elaborate. The lowest level is the decisive one, the work instruction level, serving as the yard stick for the test scripts.

When defining test data, the requirements of test scripts have to be taken into account—especially concerning the combination of possible variations of data items (variants). From those the data contents and quality are deduced. In some cases they can be satisfied by a dump from the production data base. In this case one has to decide whether partial dumps suffice or whether the productive data base has to be uploaded in its totality. In the latter case one has to make sure that the capacity of the test system is sufficient and that expected performance will be met.

If the functions are to be tested on the basis of new data to be generated or employ new algorithms, real data often do not suffice. In these cases synthetic data have to be provided—sometimes in an initially empty data base. If more than a few dozen data records are required, the effort to build up bulk complex synthetic data has to be planned. If possible these data should be generated automatically by specially written programs.

Another aspect when selecting test data is performance. As already mentioned, negative performance should not impede acceptance procedures unnecessary. On the other hand there could be special test scripts explicitly designed to test the performance of certain functions. This is obviously then the case when for example performance considerations are behind re-designs of the data model in the first place.

3.3.4   Overall Planning of Acceptance Tests Together with the Supplier

An important implementation project normally rests on an overall project plan agreed upon by all sides with all tasks and mile stones. Software acceptance as part of a complete release does appear only as a single mile stone, other acceptance objects do not appear at all—only if they represent strategic business functions. This means that, when acceptance time comes near, detailed scheduling on a day by day basis has to be drawn up. Since supplier resources have to be included close consultation taking into account his interests is indispensible.

Acceptance planning does not only deal with start and end dates for example regarding system provisioning and the testing period itself, but has to consider every function to be tested with all necessary specialist resources. Certain constellations may require that parallel testing of specific functions accessing one and the same data base has to be avoided (competing accesses, locking, risk of corrupting the data base etc.). For these cases separate time windows have to be provided. The resulting schedule, which initially is binding for the complete testing period, assigns specific functions and time windows to every resource. During acceptance testing itself, however, adjournments occasionally have to be considered because of follow-up tests, after error amendments have been carried out.

The exact format of an acceptance schedule itself is of minor importance. Only when extensive software is to be tested for the first time a thoroughly time-phased project plan should be drawn up. But also for such a case parts of it can be presented in simple EXCEL© sheets. The important things are clarity and ease of update.

3.3.5   Management of Acceptance Procedures

This core responsibility requires the agreement of all parties concerned: business units, project and supplier. Furthermore, backing and early communication has to come from top management. On top, the responsible quality manager should be a socially and professionally respected person, possessing assertiveness as well as diplomatic skill to handle compromises. It is important to provide satisfactory software solutions in good quality and in time and thus be able to pay the supplier his due. This is the common objective, which should not be impeded by a drive to perfection without compromises.

3.3.6   Final Evaluation with Recommendations

Prior to developing software there has to be an order for realisation unless the software is bought off the market shelf by the customer. Normally orders usually take on the form of a contract. This contract describes the specifics of delivery and other characteristics of the software as well as modes of payment. This contract thus presents a document of legal relevance.

The settlement of the delivered product can follow directly with reference to the contract, once all agreed upon details have been met. Auditors require that the delivery has to be documented in one form or another. This is done most appropriately at that place and at that time, when the correctness of the delivery is assessed—in our case at the end of acceptance procedures by a proper protocol.

Details will be discussed further down. However, one has to differentiate between a rather technical validation by an acceptance protocol with error documentation and a conclusion on this basis with a view on a recommendation how to deal with the results. Both points of view may of course be included in one and the same document. The final evaluation of acceptance tests will thus cover references to the acceptance objects, to acceptance procedures and a documentation of the results including error protocols. Furthermore it may contain only one out of two possible conclusions:

- Not accepted or
- Accepted.

Concerning the latter, qualifying understandings can be included. They may contain obligations, only under which the acceptance is valid. In most cases this concerns measures agreed upon between customer and supplier to amend few but important software errors not having been resolved up to the end of testing.

3.4   Basics for Acceptance Procedures

Let us first consider some conventions and rules.

3.4.1   Dates for Provisioning

One has to differentiate between three different provisioning dates:

- PfT = Provisioning for Tests.
  This is the date after the preliminary end of all development work. The developers hand over their results to the internal quality management of the supplier. Included are technical test scripts, which are necessary to test the functional features of the software. The software either resides on the various individual development systems or on a common configuration expressly conceived for internal acceptance tests (factory approval). Tests are carried out with synthetic data. The participation of the customer is formally not required, but may be of use for practical reasons. As soon as functional errors become visible

at this early stage, it does not make sense to test the associated corresponding business functions at this stage. The PfT date is somewhat decoupled from the rest of the schedule, except that is has to precede the following two dates:

- PfA = Provisioning for Acceptance.

  This date is definitely the first day of acceptance testing with the participation of the customer. It is expected that all systems are ready, that the necessary infrastructure fits, that test scripts are available and test data uploaded. A protocol of provisioning has been drafted.

- PfO = Provisioning for putting into Operation.

  Acceptance has been granted; the final evaluation report has been drafted. The new software can be rolled out into operation. For this either a release modification with all migration details has to be scheduled or an update to be provided. The update will be uploaded during operation downtime and should be put into production thereafter. It is in the interest of the customer that the PfO date should be after acceptance, which sometimes is difficult to maintain.

3.4.2   Initialisation of Acceptance Procedures

Acceptance procedures themselves commence long before the PfT date. As soon as the functional contents of the acceptance object (request process) has been clarified quality management should initiate a kick-off meeting with all parties concerned. In this meeting the state of the specification documents is reviewed, rough scheduling regarding the acceptance process is presented and responsibilities are allocated. If possible a representative of the overall project management should be present to lend weight to the importance of the undertaking. The kick-off minutes are recorded in writing and will later be archived as part of the acceptance documentation.

3.4.3   Problem and Idea Repository

Prior to the PfA date two exchange media have to be created in the acceptance account:

- A problem repository and
- An idea repository.

These tools, which can be either Word or EXCEL© tables, are at the disposition for all participants of the test team in write modus. The access path is to be communicated before hand.

All errors identified during acceptance tests or other functional problems are to be documented in the problem repository—with priorities assigned to them initially according to the subjective error criteria of the tester. The problem repository will later serve as the basis for regular acceptance reviews, during which the entries will be qualified.

All other requests and wishes for improvement as well as other observations coming to the mind of the testers during acceptance tests with a view to improve the software are to be logged in the idea repository (process: change management). By definition these thus are **not** errors. Furthermore it is quite possible that during the review process some entries qualified initially as errors may be moved from the problem to the idea repository.

Both repositories—for problems and ideas—will be closed after the completion of acceptance tests and archived as part of the acceptance documentation.

SAP offers its own error management tool, the Solution Manager. This product as well as others available from other suppliers shall not be discussed here.

3.4.4 Review Process

With the start of acceptance testing, sometimes even before the end of the first day of action, but certainly after first test results are obtained, acceptance reviews take place on a day to day basis, if possible, at a fixed time of day with the participation of the complete test team. This committee tracks and controls acceptance testing and how it progresses. During the final review the overall success of the acceptance process will be decided upon and a recommendation drafted accordingly. Such reviews usually do not take up more than half an hour's time—except at the beginning and the end of acceptance testing.

3.4.5 Patch Cycle

Right from the kick-off, when milestones have been agreed upon, the quality management of the supplier should be drawn in to draw up a schedule with the exact days of the week, when software amendments after corrections of errors having been detected during acceptance tests (process: error management) should be uploaded as patches (written agreement). The prior knowledge of the exact dates is important for re-scheduling of test resources during acceptance procedures.

3.4.6 Follow-Up Tests

It makes sense to carve up the total time frame available for testing into a time window for acceptance tests proper and a smaller one for successive follow-up tests—something to the ratio of 2:1 on the time scale. The objective is to complete all acceptance tests during the first time interval, such that during the second part only corrections have to be re-tested. However, this is sometimes difficult to maintain, because the acceptance time slot in many cases is too short because of time pressure when scheduling backwards from the PfO date, so that some functions to be tested may trail behind for acceptance testing proper right into the second time slot dedicated to re-testing. However, initial scheduling should respect this basic differentiation to aim for a minimum of discipline.

3.4.7   Detailed Tasks During Acceptance Testing

The following discussion takes into account, what has been said about responsibilities and conventions so far.

Pre-condition for the kick-off is that the functional scope to be tested is known. Functional and technical specifications have been approved. A patch cycle has also been communicated. Now the planning options as displayed in Figs. 3.2 and 3.3 can be considered.

The pivotal point is the PfA date. Assumed is a duration for acceptance proper of three calendar weeks (example), that final week of which is reserved for re-tests. Backwards there is the necessity that the system environment has to be provided not later than 1 week prior to the beginning of the acceptance process. This buffer is required since when uploading software and test data technical problems cannot be excluded. Furthermore the test data to be created have to be known not later than 1 week before system installation. The drafting of test scripts takes time. Figure 3.2 provides 4 weeks for this. This, however, is the minimum required. This initial phase could be longer.

Up front there is little slack left. Figure 3.3 displays two hypothetical upload dates for patches. The first week is out of the question since tests have just started and programming corrections will take up a finite time as well. Since quite often the PfO date is fixed closely after acceptance it is almost impossible to move re-testing further into the future.

Bearing this scheduling in mind during the kick-off the following agreements should be reached:

- Fine tuning over time of the allocation of customer resources to test script writing/test data definition and participation in the acceptance tests proper,
- Written requests regarding system and development support by the supplier on precise dates
- Request for the test environment in detail.

The test scripts themselves can be documented according to the template of Table 3.3.

There should be at least one further consultation meeting between kick-off and the PfA date with all parties concerned checking the state of acceptance preparation—preferably close to the PfA date. This will be the last opportunity to

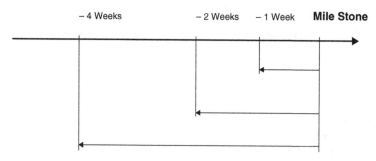

Fig. 3.2 Backwards planning

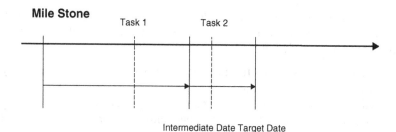

Fig. 3.3 Forward planning

escalate to project management or to the supplier, if there is a risk for certain pre-conditions not be met.

Equally, before the start of acceptance procedures the acknowledgement of the system provided should formally take place in the presence of the operator of the test system, to be documented by a protocol. The template for such a protocol is provided in Sect. 3.5.

The daily reviews during acceptance testing deal basically with the entries in the problem repository (see Table 3.1).

The individual items mean:

- Nb.: sequential number with respect to this acceptance event only, starting with a "1"
- Tester: person having noted the problem and logged it
- Problem Description: preferably elaborate description of the problem; circumstances under which it appeared; error description, if necessary supported by screen shots (appendix)
- Error Category: classification of the error after consultation with the review group
- Patch Date: planned amendment and dispatch during the current acceptance period or a future correction date for not so important errors
- Status: working status of error correction:

Table 3.1 Problem repository

No.	Tester	Problem description	Error category	Patch date	Status

- Open
- Analysed
- Work in progress
- To be delivered
- Dispatched
- Re-tested.

Prioritisation is important. Contrary to the subjective feeling of a tester the review meetings should come to objective assessments, which problems accepted as errors are to be classified in the following way:

- Production prohibiting: die function produces wrong results, breaks down, follows a logic, which is unusable etc. (Prio 1)
- Production prohibiting, but can be used on a temporary basis by employing a workaround (the duration of the workaround until the error to be fixed has to be agreed upon) (Prio 2)
- All other errors (Prio 3).

If test sequences make it necessary a fall-back schedule should be prepared. Such an eventuality makes sense, when it is to be expected that the test environment may become unstable (data overruns, table overruns, other system failures) and has to be re-initialised. The time available in our example covering only 3 weeks, limits this possibility significantly.

The acceptance protocol should contain the following elements:

- Date
- Acceptance object, if necessary reference to an order
- Functions in detail (mention—not full description)
- Configuration for the acceptance tests
- Types of test data
- Persons responsible (sub-project leaders)
- Names of the testers
- Results per function (accepted y/n or conditionally)
- Remaining errors and mutually agreed correction dates
- General recommendation.

3.4.8   Operational Readiness and Pilot Operation

Our discussions up to now have assumed that the acceptance procedures for a given release should suffice to clear software for regular operation and production. For highly complex systems with many interfaces and individual modules to be tested separately demands are higher. In this case the customer requires a higher degree of security. To meet this, an additional operational readiness check, including or not a pilot operation phase, may be provided.

3.4.8.1   Operational Readiness Check

The aim is to make sure that all services necessary for the deployment of a system as ordered by the customer have been provided by the supplier and are ready for operation. This may include more than just software: In addition there may be:

- Utilities necessary to support production
- Access security concepts
- Multi-client capability
- Separate standard reporting facilities
- Documentation
- In certain cases production schedules and operating system support
- Hotline and other support functions.

Since all functional tests have been passed already at this point in time the operational readiness check need no longer include those. A stock taking of the overall organisational, technical and operational situation for a given date should suffice. This will be documented separately (see template "Operational Readiness Declaration" under Sect. 3.5).

3.4.8.2   Pilot Operation

Equally, for pilot operations dedicated tests are no longer required, since acceptance procedures will have come to an end. But prior to it operational readiness checks as outlined above should have been done. The type of pilot operation depends on the deployment philosophy initially agreed upon. It therefore could for example take place on a parallel system. This is recommended in case that the existing production configuration has to be migrated only. The disadvantage is that for a realistic pilot operation the complete production environment with all its operational facets has to be mapped, all professional resources being usually employed in daily business have to be recruited.

Another possibility is the monitoring of the productive system (after acceptance!) under load. The disadvantage is obvious: it resides in the risk starting operations with all business processes without prior rehearsal. In practice one has to define two reference dates: beginning and end. During production system behaviour should be recorded and evaluated with respect to performance and appearance of errors for this logically defined period. Such a pilot operation may last for several months. At the same time production is continuing. Severe deficiencies would pop up with high probability already shortly after the start date. For this reason a water tight fall-back strategy with short reaction times should be devised.

3.5   Templates

The following templates are useful: Responsibility Table (Table 3.2), Test Scripts (Table 3.3), Acceptance Protocol, Task List (Fig. 3.4), Problem Repository (Fig. 3.5), Idea Repository (Fig. 3.6), Protocol of System Provisioning (Table 3.4) Operational Readiness Check (Table 3.5).

Table 3.2   Responsibilities

Role	Name	Business unit
Direction	Representative of Supplier for example	
Direction	Representative of Client	
	QM Manager Client	
	QM Manager Supplier	
	Consultant	
	Controller	
Role	Name	Business unit
Tester	Tester1	
Tester	Tester2	
Tester	. . ..	
Tester	TesterN	

Table 3.3   Test scripts

Sub-Process Level 1	
Sub-Process Level 2	
Work Instruction	
Cont. No.	
Variant	
Input	
Output	
Acceptance Criteria	

- Sub-Process Level 1 (acc. Fig. 3.1)
- Sub-Process Level 2 (acc. Fig. 3.1)
- Work Instruction: smallest process step regarding for example data entry for a business scenario
- Cont. No.: unequivocal identification number for each variant of the work instruction, generated usually from the process hierarchy (for example 1.2.3.4)
- Variant: referring to different initial situations of a particular work instruction, for example referring to different customer segments, when entering a contract
- Input: batch or online
- Output: expected output after executing a particular algorithm, a sort or a listing etc.
- Acceptance Criteria: additional criteria other than "output" (for example locking accesses to certain data, performance etc.)

Acceptance Protocol: Software xyz—Version n.m

Author:
Distribution List:
Acceptance Date:

Contents

1. Objectives
2. Acceptance Procedure for Software xyz
3. Participants
4. Acceptance Objects
5. Result
6. Acceptance Statement

1. Objectives

The present document summarises the results of the acceptance tests for system xyz, Release n.m.

2. Acceptance Procedure for Software xyz

- The software package xyz has been made available for acceptance tests at the mm.dd.yyyy to the customer ABC.
- Aim and purpose of the acceptance tests for this system were to verify, whether all project objectives and requests for the software system delivered have been fulfilled, by mutual agreement.
- Criteria for the assessment of the degree of fulfilment were test scenarios agreed upon by the customer ABC and the supplier DEF, which were provided as a basis for systematic and thorough testing.
- The mutually agreed acceptance procedures are laid down in the document "Acceptance Specification xyz Version n.m". Important changes/corrections were documented in agreement protocols and implemented in time.

- Once the system xyz n.m meets the acceptance criteria at the end of the acceptance period, the customer will formally declare his acceptance of the system.
- Should the acceptance criteria not be met by 100 %, acceptance can be declared conditionally. The constraints have to be documented.
- After acceptance the project will amend known errors in sequence of their priorities right after going productive. During acceptance procedures error amendments (patches) should have been introduced already.
- The acceptance configuration was provided including servers with the following utilities:

  - ....

- The acceptance configuration for system xyz was provided by .... in <location, postal address> in the premises of the customer ABC.
- Dates: start of acceptance tests: <mm.dd.yyyy>
- End of acceptance tests: <mm.dd.yyyy>

The acceptance test results are shown under list item 5 (Acceptance Results Rel_n.m) in detail.

Errors recorded by the customer ABC are described in an error protocol with their respective priorities. This protocol will be handed over as soon as possible at the end of the acceptance test period to the supplier DEF. It may contain a declaration of acceptance refusal, a possible justification for the refusal and the final error protocol.

Errors are prioritised in the following way:

- Production prohibiting: die function produces wrong results, breaks down, follows a logic, which is unusable etc. (Prio 1)
- Production prohibiting, but can be used on a temporary basis by employing a workaround (the duration of the workaround until the error to be fixed has to be agreed upon) (Prio 2)
- All other errors (Prio 3).

At the end of the various acceptance phases the list of identified errors is the basis for a final evaluation. During this process errors, which had already been amended during this acceptance phase, are marked as corrected since they had been quality assured by the supplier.

Acceptance of the system xyz is granted, if at the end of the acceptance test period at <mm.dd.yyyy> no errors remain, which are bound to impede the proper functioning of the system.

Errors of priority 2 and 3 remaining after acceptance tests will be fixed during productive operation according to an agreed upon schedule as fast as possible.

Requests formulated during the acceptance test period will be handled by request/change management of the project xyz and documented in the daily review protocols.

3. Participants
see Template Table 3.2.

4. Acceptance Objects
All modules of the delivery are detailed in the document "Acceptance Specification xyz Version n.m".

5. Results
Number and Priority of Errors by Test Case:

Component	Test Case	Prio 1	Prio 2	Prio 3	Remarks
Divers	Tracker Entries				
	Error Total				

List of Errors Known Beforehand:

Short description	Priority	Status	Object

Evaluation and Acceptance Status

A = without fault

B = accepted under the condition "amendment asap" (fixing of errors is managed transparently via a tracker and will be quality assured by the supplier)

C = not accepted

Acceptance object	Acceptance status
Software System xyz n.m	

6. Acceptance by the Ordering Party
The acceptance of the acceptance objects outlined above is granted after thorough review of the documents provided and the test results obtained.

The results and evaluations of this acceptance test are recorded in list item 5 "Results" (with some possible constraints) and logged in the tracker.

Date   Acceptance Manager

Task	Responsible	Target Date	Status
accept software	Myers	130912	done
check data	Reynolds	131130	in progress

Fig. 3.4 Task list

No.	Tester	Test Case No.	Problem Description	Priority	Date	Status

Fig. 3.5 Problem repository

No.	Tester	Work Instruction / Sub-Process	Change Request	Date

Fig. 3.6 Idea repository

Table 3.4 Provisioning protocol

System Component	State
Server Configuration	
Periphery	
Disk Drives	
Data Base	
System Programs	
Communication Programs	
Software to be tested	
Other Utility Programs	
Customising	
Logfiles	
Responsible Acceptance Manager	

Table 3.5 Operational
readiness check

No.	Object	Status/comment
•	System Components	
	Server Configuration Periphery Software System Software Customising Utility Programs Data Base	
	Initial Upload/Migrations	
	Cyclical Interfaces	
	Standard Reports	
	Trainings held	
	Documentation	

3.6   Approach

Agreement of objectives between supplier and customer > identification of specific test requirements > allocation of test responsibilities > definition of tests scripts and test data > scheduling, execution, evaluation > preparation of error documentation > controlling the review process > definition of patch cycle > if necessary pilot operation.

Chapter 4
Quality Management as a Sub-project

4.1 Project Environment

Additionally to defining tasks and the overall project organisation it is indispensible to equip the project itself with sufficient instruments so that responsibilities remain transparent and frictional losses at all execution levels are minimised. Some of the most important aspects in an implementation project are efficient communication paths and documenting the project progress. Escalation paths are part of all communication procedures. Documentation means consolidated progress reports for management, but also recording work progress in detail.

To maintain communication and documentation in consultation with all responsible parties appropriate organisational and technical structures have to be implemented—prior to project launch. With a view on technical possibilities there exist a multitude of tools on offer today from the vast pool of office and web technologies. This leads to a freedom of choice, which is not meant to be restricted by the following proposals. In the end, type and capabilities of the instruments to be used are of secondary importance, if only the objectives of the tasks at hand will be met.

4.2 Communication and Documentation

4.2.1 Routine Communication

There exist several processes with respect to routine communication important to an acceptance project. Basically one distinguishes between internal and external communication. Internally communication paths are responsible for the dissemination of information within the sub-project "Quality Management". External communication deals both with reporting to the overall project management and informing line management about important developments.

© Springer-Verlag Berlin Heidelberg 2014
W.W. Osterhage, *IT Quality Management*, DOI 10.1007/978-3-662-43767-4_4

4.2.1.1 Sub-project Internal Communication

Early on in the acceptance process a kick-off is organised. Sub-project management has been informed about the functional contents of the acceptance object and the most important milestones. From the acceptance object and content the necessary professional competences of the testers can be deduced. These are quite often people who have participated in drafting the functional specifications. Project management addresses the responsible department heads and asks for the temporary release for the duration of acceptance testing of the identified resources or alternative persons deemed to be useful for the task. In this way the fist members of the kick-off from the business units are to be selected.

Prior to kick-off acceptance management and its counterpart on the supplier side should consult each other to fix communication rules for the event. They have to agree in particular upon possible critical stress situations to be expected. This obviously depends strongly on the type of functions to be tested: interfaces, changes to the data architecture, chaining of batch runs etc. After clarification of these boundary conditions the kick-off can take place—normally several weeks before the start of the acceptance procedures themselves.

All persons carrying at least some responsibilities, sub-project management, contact persons from the supplier during acceptance tests, other specialists and—if possible—a representative of request management as well as representatives of the ordering party either from business units or the IT line organisation should be present. During the kick-off the following issues have to be clarified:

- Allocation of responsible testers to individual functions.
- Test data required (dumps from the productive systems or synthetic data),
- Interface runs
- Business processes to be tested—test scripts (to be drafted or distributed),
- User access rights
- Test sequence scheduling
- Patch cycle
- Review cycle.

The results are to be recorded in a protocol and to be communicated to the participants and the hierarchy. Sometimes there will be an additional intermediate meeting prior to acceptance tests or working groups to work out specific details such as test scripts etc.

During the acceptance tests regular reviews take place. As already mentioned above they are used to

- Prioritise errors
- Schedule patch deliveries
- Adjust the schedule
- Work out issues to be clarified
- Formulate new change requests.

The final review before the end of the acceptance phase serves to decide whether and under which conditions acceptance can be recommended.

4.2.1.2 External Routine Communication

To overall project management:

The overall project management under which quality management functions only as a sub-project normally consolidates all sub-project reports and therefore expects a status for each mile stone at fixed intervals: weekly or bi-weekly in most cases. Details from the phase prior to kick-off and from reviews are less interesting. Expected are:

• Progress on critical tasks
• Risks to project objectives,
• Risks to the project budget,
• Decision proposals.

To line management:

Line managers expect assurance regarding the time schedule for putting the announced functions into service with the quality required. In most cases acceptance management will be invited to regular meetings to report on the topic. Reporting format can be identical as that for overall management.

Escalation paths:

Since problems can have different origins different escalation paths may apply:

• Resource bottlenecks concerning testers (heads of business units),
• System availability and support (supplier hierarchy),
• Risks concerning the schedule (overall project management),
• Other.

For reasons of efficiency, however, it makes sense to define a single escalation path for all problem types in the first place—and this should normally and initially to the overall project management. In the end all paths will end up at top management anyway to which both line and project have to report.

4.2.2 Documentation

The documentation of test scripts has already been discussed in this book.

This section deals with the documentation of project preparation and project progress. All relevant documents should be posted online in a separate directory with read and write accesses depending on the role of a person in the project.

It is useful to prepare special acceptance guidelines (see Chap. 5). This directive covers all agreements from the request phase up to operational readiness.

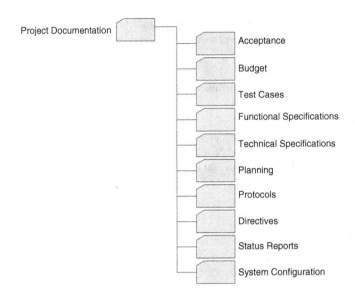

Fig. 4.1 Documentation structure

Additionally a documentation structure should be created to record project progress. An example structure is presented in Fig. 4.1.

In any case it should cover the following key aspects to be taken into account, depending on the type of project:

- Acceptance directive
- Other directives
- Schedule
- Functional specifications
- Technical specifications
- Test scripts
- System configuration
- Budget
- Protocols
- Status reports
- Acceptance results.

The main directory again is broken up into sub-structures as shown in the example of Fig. 4.2 for different applications:

4.2.2.1 Technical Specification Phase

Special emphasis should be placed on the technical specification phase. Some schools call technical specifications also business blueprints although the meaning is not quite identical. We will not discuss these differences here. As already

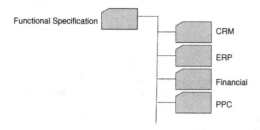

Functional Specification

CRM

ERP

Financial

PPC

Fig. 4.2 Application break-down

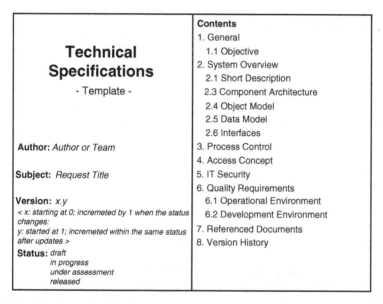

Technical Specifications

- Template -

Author: *Author or Team*

Subject: *Request Title*

Version: *x.y*
< x: starting at 0; incremeted by 1 when the status changes:
y: started at 1; incremeted within the same status after updates >
Status: *draft*
in progress
under assessment
released

Contents
1. General
   1.1 Objective
2. System Overview
   2.1 Short Description
   2.3 Component Architecture
   2.4 Object Model
   2.5 Data Model
   2.6 Interfaces
3. Process Control
4. Access Concept
5. IT Security
6. Quality Requirements
   6.1 Operational Environment
   6.2 Development Environment
7. Referenced Documents
8. Version History

Fig. 4.3 Technical specifications 1

explained the technical specifications are the basis for test scripts and thus serve as a yardstick for the acceptance as such (as an example for their contents structure see Figs. 4.3, 4.4, 4.5, 4.6 and 4.7).

In many cases for updates (release, service pack) several different functional specifications may be needed: each for a specific functional change or enhancement. These documents are sometimes cleared by completely different persons—depending on the required professional knowledge. Furthermore these documents will not be circulated all at the same time but one at a time. This means that the sub-project has to provide for a tracking mechanism. The tracking management communicates between the authors of the technical specifications from the supplier and the clearing body from the customer. Its aim is to achieve clearance early enough so that there remains sufficient time for realisation to keep the acceptance date. In this phase, however, there may still be change requests from the business units coming in once they see their requests in writing for the first time. The tracking management should then take care about such requests and how to deal with them.

1. General	2. System Overview
1.1 Objective	2.1 Short Description
The technical specifications describe the solutions by which functional requests are to be implemented. A detailed system description is the basis for the realisation by the developpers of the supplier.	*The application, main functions and the system platform to be employed.*
	2.2 Component Architecture
The requests laid down in the functional specifications are to be translated into technical solutions and their pre-conditions.	*Either using existing structures or creating new ones with new functions.*
	Interplay between the various system components and their mutual dependencies.

Fig. 4.4 Technical specifications 2

2.3 Object Model	2.5 Interfaces
Taking into account the component architecture the individual object models are to be developped, supplemented or left as they are and tailored to suit the new architecture.	*The interface description contains information about data items to be exchanged and their formats, plausibility checks, mapping tables, access modes etc.*
2.4 Data Model	*Should interface descriptions be available already in separate documents these could be referenced.*
Translation of the object models into a physical data structure with data base schema, tables and attributes as a basis for the implementation of the modified data base.	

Fig. 4.5 Technical specifications 3

3. Process Control	5. IT Security
Decision how to trigger the application (sychronous, asynchronous), imbedding into the workflow, sequencing of input screens etc.	*Identification of suitable tools, system components and physical requirements which guarantee the requested standard in the functional specifications.*
4. Access Concept	**6. Quality Requirements**
As laid down in the functional specifications, access paths and attributes as well as profiles are to be implemented in tables.	6.1 Operational Configuration
	Description of the configuration necessary for the operation of the software.
	6.2 Development Environment
	Technical development standards, tools, interface simulations, test data, release process, configuration parameters

Fig. 4.6 Technical specifications 4

7. Referenced Documents	8. Version History
All documents of importance necessary to understand the functional requests:	*The following template is useful:*
-*functional specifications* -*predecessor of technical specifications in the context of the current project* -*process documentation* -*object models* -*meeting minuts* -*error protocols*	

Version	Status	Date	Responsible	Remarks

Fig. 4.7 Technical specifications 5

4.3 Structures

The sub-project "Quality Management" has to be established once a critical size of the tasks ahead has been reached. Contents and responsibilities have to be defined in detail and allocated to different function owners if necessary. The following areas have to be attended to:

- General administration
- Project management; tool
- Documentation
- Scheduling and control
- Reporting
- Budget management
- Acceptance procedures
- Acceptance results.

It is not necessary to install a separate manager for each of these areas. Quite often certain tasks can be attended to by one and the same resource, for example administration and the deployment of project management tools. It is important that responsibilities have been defined and work contents taken into account. In regular team meetings (not in the acceptance reviews, however!) work progress has to be reported and serve as a basis for consolidated reporting to higher levels.

4.4 Mapping of Project Structures

The detailed structure of responsibilities with its work content can be mapped perfectly to a directory structure residing on a dedicated logical disk drive. An example structure is shown in Fig. 4.8.

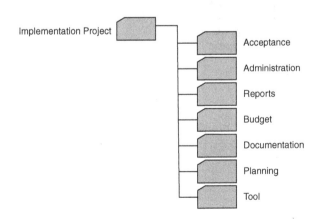

Fig. 4.8 Project structure

4.4.1 Budget Planning

Without budget (in sight) no project can start. The highest level relevant to controlling is the overall budget with just one figure behind it and which may not be exceeded at the end of the project. But in most cases this budget is broken down into an investment (hardware) part and into a personnel cost plan. The personnel cost plan is spread over the time line of the project and details requested and granted project days per unit time (in most cases per month) per project resource. For each day's contingency corresponding daily rates in money are allocated. In this way bottlenecks and—from feedback via time sheets—project days not used up can be tracked. A regular re-planning during project progress is usually required.

4.5 Templates

The following templates are useful: Kick-off Agenda (Fig. 4.9), Test Schedule (Fig. 4.10), Patch Cycle (Fig. 4.11) and Status Report (Fig. 4.12).

Agenda Acceptance Tests Kick-off

- Introduction
- Presentation of Schedule
- Explanation of Test Process
- Assigning Tester to Test Cases
- Identification of Test Data
- Technical Pre-conditions
- Review Process
- Patch Cycle
- Access Rights

Fig. 4.9 Kick-off agenda

Step No.	Date	Time	Batch Description	Result	Evaluation

Fig. 4.10 Test schedule

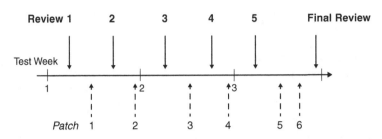

Fig. 4.11 Patch cycle

Project Status: Project Name   **Date of Report:**

Mile Stone	Degree of Completion	Problems	Measures
Designation Task1 Task2			
Designation Task1 Task2			
Designation Task1 Task2			
Designation Task1 Task2			

Fig. 4.12 Status report

4.6 Approach

Detailed description of the sub-project environment > installation of regular communication and reporting as well as escalation paths > definition of documentation structure > mapping of individual responsibilities within the sub-project structure > budget planning and controlling.

Chapter 5
Acceptance Directive

5.1 Justification

From the discussion so far it is obvious that various interested parties take part in test and acceptance procedures. The more important partners are:

- Supplier (and his development department as well as his internal quality assurance team)
- Customer
- Project management.

  On the customer side:

- Business units
- IT organisation.

Regarding the overall project organisation IT quality management is the most important sub-project, but other players include:

- Request management
- Change management
- IT security and others.

It has proven useful not only to regularise the different interests and responsibilities for software acceptance by contract but—based on practical experience—to summarise them also in another common document: an Acceptance Directive. This directive should be tailored to the specific acceptance scenario and can always be referred to in cases of conflict. Its most important advantage is that right from the beginning of the process the roles for all participants are clearly defined. These preliminary clarifications and their successive codification in a directive will save many frictional losses and later clarification discussions. The directive can serve furthermore as a blueprint for future acceptance tests and can be adjusted accordingly.

© Springer-Verlag Berlin Heidelberg 2014
W.W. Osterhage, *IT Quality Management*, DOI 10.1007/978-3-662-43767-4_5

5.2   Relationship Between the Contract Partners

Obviously different partners stand for different interests. The supplier's objective is to deliver his order in time and obtain acceptance with a view to receive a timely payment and a minimum of warranty commitments. The business units would like to get the functions requested, whereby the expectations between supplier and business may diverge. In some cases the end user recognises only after realisation, what had really been on his mind, but had then been specified in a way that the supplier may have misinterpreted the functional specifications. These conflicts have to be resolved during acceptance tests. Professional technical know how and management competences of the project leadership will prove to be decisive factors.

The customer's IT organisation has to deal with follow up activities after acceptance such as putting the system into operation and support the production by a service centre. It is therefore important to make sure that there is mutual agreement between business units and IT on these matters regarding the necessary service mentality. Similar considerations concern the roles of the sub-projects request management, change management, security and others, which quite often tend to hide behind administrative rules governing their work.

Project management has to make sure that all participants manoeuvre towards a common goal. In the end the objective is the same for all: mutual satisfaction. For this reason it will be inevitable that during the acceptance process compromises and accommodations will be required from all sides. This goes well beyond the limits of any formal agreement.

5.3   Finding Consensus

The directive should be written by acceptance coordination, i.e. drafted by the customer's quality management. As will be shown further on, all basic aspects but also many operational details are to be documented. Subsequently the document should undergo a clearing process, the history of which is to be recorded. It should be released under the participation of at least one representative of the supplier—in certain circumstances also by department heads of the customer. It serves as a reference for the overall project management and is the working basis for the sub-project management.

Thus its creation follows an iterative process. The result can be archived together with the rest of contract documents.

5.4 The Directive

5.4.1 Introduction

5.4.1.1 Scope of the Document

Acceptance for system xyz is generally laid down in the document "Acceptance Directive, Principles Regarding Organisation and Procedures".

The present document presents the acceptance specification for the acceptance phase "Release n.1" by the client and concerns the functional scope agreed upon previously and laid down in the corresponding technical specifications. These technical specifications were written on the basis of the relevant business processes and have been documented in "Test Case Catalogue for the Acceptance of System xyz Release n.1".

The basis for acceptance is the technical specifications. Additional work documents which have been consulted to draft the specifications are referenced further down. The ranking of importance follows the sequence in the list.

The QS internal processes of the supplier relevant for acceptance are outlined in the document "Acceptance Procedures xyz_Rel_n.1".

5.4.1.2 Specific Scope

This document is valid for the acceptance test and its results concerning the project with the same name xyz by the client with reference to the acceptance object "xyz Version n.1".

This object has been agreed upon by the client and the system supplier previously and continues to be valid in its actual version.

Individual aspects of this specification can be subject to alterations during acceptance tests for organisational or procedural reasons. As long as they are recorded in mutually agreed upon protocols these are legitimate parts of the acceptance specification.

5.4.2 Definition of Terms

5.4.2.1 Acceptance

Acceptance in the premises of the supplier succeeds the phases of test case definitions by the customer as part of the test process and amendments after system development. The latter had been finalised with a quality assured release for delivery. Its objective is to prove the overall fully functional operation as a pre-condition for putting it into production (as a pre-condition for implementation).

Emphasis of acceptance is on the assessment of functional completeness regarding the functional specifications with respect to its basis, the relevant business processes.

Basis and procedures of test case implementation as well as test process steps will be discussed in a separate section.

The total acceptance procedure has to be completed within ten work days. At the end of each work day a review takes place with the participation of members of a steering group for error validation (criteria see below).

The amendment of critical errors takes place twice after each Wednesday by the development team. The patches created for this will be cleared and uploaded on the following Thursday. Thereafter a re-test of the previously erroneous functions takes place. The only other documentation tool besides the protocol forms of the test persons is the error tracker used by the supplier.

Further amendments of non-critical errors or deficiencies will be handled by the existing error and configuration management.

Acceptance of the system xyz n.1 can be pronounced when at the end of the acceptance phase on date mm.dd.yyyy no errors remain which might substantially impede the implementation project.

5.4.3   Contributions

Both supplier and customer have to provide certain contributions according to the task allocations below. For this purpose a steering group and an acceptance team are to be created taking over part of the tasks of supplier and customer.

The supplier has to take care of the following tasks in the context of acceptance procedures:

- Provisioning of acceptance readiness
- Provisioning of a functioning test system (including installed software)
- Provisioning of all system components undergoing acceptance tests
- Delivery of the complete software and its documentation on a suitable medium
- Implementation of customising requirements from the customer
- Provisioning of test data having been identified together with the customer
- If necessary, provisioning of additional support regarding computing and service centre
- Provisioning of acceptance test resources to support for example the test configuration for the acceptance team.
- Definition of a detailed acceptance test schedule
- Shared management of the acceptance team together with the customer
- Provide staff to participate in acceptance tests
- Training of the acceptance team to enable them to carry out acceptance tests and operate the system

- Manage errors and deliver amendments of the software within an agreed time period.

The customer has to take care of the following task in the context of acceptance procedures:

- Provide staff to participate in the steering group
- Provide staff to participate in the acceptance test team
- Write test cases including acceptance criteria
- Specify customising requests to the supplier
- Shared management of the steering group with the supplier
- Shared management of the acceptance team with the supplier
- Work out test data requirements with the supplier
- Transformation of test cases into test process steps together with the supplier.

From the above mentioned tasks the steering group is responsible for the following:

- Installation of the acceptance team,
- Resource planning,
- Management of all preparations for acceptance tests in compliance with the acceptance specification and acceptance test schedule as well as initiating and tracking of suitable measures in case of departure from the task list,
- Evaluation of acceptance test results to be formally approved by the signatures of the common sub-project management on the acceptance protocol,
- Clarifying conflicting interpretations of acceptance test results and escalate these issues if necessary,
- Initiate measures for error amendments and track them.

From the above mentioned tasks the acceptance test team is responsible for the following:

- Participation in the training
- Carry out acceptance tests with test protocols and enter error messages in the error tracking tool
- Daily review about acceptance tests with recommendations for follow up measures
- Test reports to the steering group.

5.4.4   Acceptance Readiness and Time Schedule

At the start of acceptance procedures the test system will be provided and the components to be accepted documented in a protocol of provisioning (see appendix). The acceptance test team checks the system whether it is correctly set up with respect to the requirements indicated in the section about reference documents.

Missing pre-conditions are to be recorded in the protocol and checked against possible impairment of acceptance readiness. Once all conditions have been met the acceptance team declares acceptance test readiness and records it in the protocol of provisioning. The acceptance team decides upon possible measures necessary to establish acceptance test readiness.

The relevant dates for acceptance are the following:

June 30 2015	Delivery Software xyz n.1
July 1st 2015	Provision of Acceptance Criteria
August 12 2015	Provisioning Training System
August 16 2015	Provisioning Test Cases and Test Data for Acceptance
August 19 2015	Provisioning Software for Acceptance Testing
August 30 2015	Acceptance

5.4.4.1   Partial Acceptance

Some components and their specific features of system xyz can be checked by different dedicated acceptance tests. They are:

- User functions
- Access rights
- Simulated interface functions.

5.4.5   Set Up of the Tests

5.4.5.1   Basic Principles

The overall test scenario is based on two pillars:

- Dissection of the main process xyz into clearly identified and identifiable test cases,
- Transformation of these test cases into separate test process steps within a defined configuration and on the basis of appropriate test data.

5.4.5.2   Dissection of the Business Process xyz

The dissection of the main process follows this hierarchy:

- Sub-process level 1
- Sub-process level 2
- . . ..
- Work instruction.

On the work instruction level further scenarios with regard to the variables "start condition" and "input" are possible. The combination of these three items is uniquely identifiable by a running number following the process hierarchy.

5.4.5.3   Acceptance Criteria

For each identified test case there exist acceptance criteria, which can be differentiated as follows:

- Expected output and
- Purpose (relative to the work instruction).

5.4.5.4   Reference

Every test case with its acceptance criteria is recorded in a test case catalogue. This catalogue contains also evaluation matrices for each test case holding the following information:

- Relevance
- Test area
- Test result
- Comment
- Tester and
- Tracker ID.

(Error protocol in the appendix).

5.4.5.5   Test Process Steps

While test process steps are defined by the relevant specialist teams of developers and test case authors the supplier provides his technical test results from the development phase to the teams.

The test process steps are to be recorded in a data base as follows:

ID	> Identification
Short Text	> Break up of Test Case into Test Steps
Step 1	Description of Test Process Step 1
Step 2	Description of Test Process Step 2

Description of test data

. . ..

Mapping to the software test work flow

. . ..

Expected result

. . ..

Description of test infrastructure
(Reference to an infrastructure description, to be created initially and saved in a
    central directory, thereafter only referenced)
Test execution
Step 1:
Date:

. . ..

Result	Example: "The contract version has been updated correctly."
	> **Protocol**

5.4.6   Acceptance Object xyz n.1

5.4.6.1   Reference Documents

Relevant for acceptance are only the technical specifications starting with the
running number 1 in the table presented in Sect. 5.5. All other documents have
only a supporting role for the acceptance procedures.

5.4.7   Acceptance Object

Acceptance objects are the components of the test system as provided and
documented by the protocol of provisioning (template see Sect. 5.5).

5.4.8   Pre-conditions

5.4.8.1   Acceptance Location

Acceptance procedures take place in the premises of the supplier (address). Appropriately equipped rooms (telephone, LAN-connection, access to the test system,
work stations etc.) are to be provided.

5.4.8.2   Test System

At the start of procedures the test system requested by the steering group with
simulated interfaces and the data load identified during test step definition have to

be ready. The test system comprises basically a server configuration dedicated for tests of the production schedule and a separate server configuration for individual function tests. The software xyz n.1 has been subject to previous customising according to the demands by the customer.

The components of the provided test system are recorded in the protocol of provisioning.

5.4.8.3   Test Data

Acceptance of the acceptance object xyz version n.1 is granted on the basis of test data, which have been identified, specified and selected during the definition of the test process steps.

These data as well as the complete configuration have to be duplicated prior to the start of acceptance procedures and saved to be able to reproduce test process steps at all times under identical conditions.

5.4.9   Execution

5.4.9.1   Steering Group

(template see Sect. 5.5)

5.4.9.2   Acceptance Team

(template see Sect. 5.5)

5.4.10   Acceptance Tests

5.4.10.1   Application Functions: Integrity, Correctness

Acceptance tests of application functions assure the correctness, integrity as well as the interplay of individual basic functions on the basis of the mapping of test cases on a sequence of test process steps.

After each test process step it is recorded whether the software functions according to specification. After passing each test process step the members of the acceptance team decide about possible errors, and which priority they get assigned. Errors are to be prioritised in the following way:

- Priority 1: the error leads to production break down and cannot be circumvented.

  If this is not the case, the application function passes as accepted.

An error is classified as acceptance prohibiting, when the productive use of the software is impeded seriously because the function in question is not carried out at all or in such an erroneous way that its intended function cannot be achieved even by a work around.

During the acceptance test phase these errors have to be fixed within a controlled patch delivery schedule under the responsibility of the configuration management.

- Priority 2: the error leads to production break down but there exists a work around.
- Priority 3: the errors neither leads to production stand still nor to production impediment.

Errors of category 2 and 3 are classified as not to be acceptance prohibiting. These errors limit the operational usage of the software only in a limited way. Such errors are documented for later corrections in a follow up list in the tracking tool.

In the end the list of identified errors is subject to a final evaluation. Those errors having been amended during the acceptance test phase already are marked as corrected in as much as they have been quality assured by the internal quality management of the project. Evaluation criteria:

A	= without fault
B	= acceptance under the condition that errors will be amended (the amendment of errors is tracked by the error tracker and managed by the internal quality management)
C	= not accepted

After or during the passing of all test process steps all test results are documented. If there should be no acceptance prohibiting error at the end of the test series a protocol confirming acceptance will be provided by the steering group.

5.4.10.2   Access Rights

The access concept has to be tested on the basis of a test scenario including acceptance criteria with respect to two aspects:

- Conformity with the IT standards of the ordering party,
- Possibility to implement special user profiles with regard to specific xyz functionalities.

5.4.10.3   Interface Functions Under Simulated Conditions

Test cases and thus test process steps demand interface data and functions with regard to:

- Explicit test case functions (work instructions)
- Input from interfaces for further processing
- Output to external systems via interfaces.

In the course of transcribing test cases to test process steps the necessary data environment is generated via log files as a basis for testing the relevant functions.

5.4.11   Appendix/Checklists

5.4.11.1   Test Protocol

Every relevant action of each team is to be recorded in a protocol with date and name. These are the relevant tasks:

- Alteration/creation of test cases,
- Definition or production of test data and the dump taken from,
- Execution of a test process step with the software used and referenced to the data and the dump taken from ,
- Software error with tracker ID,
- Functional gap,
- Required contribution (see Sect. 5.4.3) provided or not,
- Other.

5.4.12   Protocol of Provisioning

(template see Sect. 5.5)

5.5   Templates

This document has been approved by:

Name	Date	Object of approval	Signature
Department Head 1		Completeness/Correctness	
Department Head 2		Completeness/Correctness	
Remitter		Completeness/Correctness	
QM Supplier		Completeness/Correctness	
Sub-Project Manager		Completeness/Correctness	
QM Customer		Completeness/Correctness	

The procedures described in this document were approved by:

Table 5.1 Clearance of acceptance directive

Approved by	Company	Date	Signature
Executive	Customer		
Executive	Supplier		

This document is only valid after clearance and signature by the above project management.

Table 5.2 Clearance history

Version	Status	Date	Responsible	Note
0.1	Intermediate			First draft
0.2	Intermediate			Revision
0.3	Intermediate			Revision
0.4	Intermediate			Revised after consultation with . . ..
1.0	Released		see above	

Table 5.3 Reference documents

No.	Filename	Author	Description	Version	Date
1	TS_xyz	Supplier	Technical specification software xyz n.m		
2	FS_xyz	Customer	Functional specification software xyz n.m		
3		Procurement	Software xyz n.m delivery contract		
4		QM customer	Acceptance directive		
5		Supplier	Development tests results		
6		Testers	Test case catalog		
7		Testers	Test protocols		
8		Supplier	Protocol of provisioning		
9		Supplier, testers	Problem repository		

Table 5.4 Acceptance objects

Component	Contents: xyz version n.m	Comment
1. Functionality	To prove the functional extent, the system components of version xyz n.m are tested on the basis of the test case catalogue based in turn on the xyz technical specification [TS_xyz]	Complete tests of all test process steps
2. Access rights	Access rights concept concerning functional and data accesses on the basis of access rights profiles	As described in the technical specification
3. Interface functions	Simulated interfaces • INT1 • INT2 • Export A • Export B • Import C • Import D •	Interfaces simulated via log files for import/export

Table 5.5 Acceptance test tasks

Acceptance tasks xyz n.m		
Acceptance measures	Date	Responsible
Acceptance Tests Announcement		Request Management
Install Steering Group Actions: • Draft schedule for acceptance tests • Install acceptance test team		Sub-Project Management
Schedule Tests for acceptance test team Actions: • Collect and verify reference documents • Coordinate test cases/test process steps • Define and provide test data • Identify acceptance criteria • Update acceptance test time schedule		Steering Group/QM Customer
Prepare acceptance test system Input: protocol of provisioning Actions: • Upload dump • Documentation xyz and patch level • Interfaces ready • Functional check • Clear day-to-day scenarios		Steering Group
Carry out partial acceptance tests Input: • Test process steps • Time schedule • Individual functions • Access rights concept Output: tracker, test reports, problem repository Actions: Proceed through test process steps		All

Table 5.6 Responsibilities

Role	Name	Unit
Manager	Example: representative of supplier	
Manager	Ex. representative of customer	
	Ex. QM Manager Customer	
	Ex. QM Manager Supplier	
	Ex. consultant	
	Ex. controller	
Tester	Tester1	
Tester	Tester2	
Tester	. . ..	
Tester	TesterN	

Table 5.7 Protocol of provisioning

System component	Status
Server Configuration	
Periphery	
Disks	
Data Base	
System Programs	
Communication Programs	
Software to be accepted	
Other Utilities	
Customising	
Logfiles	
Responsible for Acceptance	

5.6   Approach

Identification of interest groups > inspire common understanding > define objectives > draft directive > take business decisions > bring about agreements > implement directive.

Chapter 6
Methods of Data and Software Migration

6.1 Acceptance Procedures and Data

In many cases, when implementing new systems, a data base, either entirely new or from a predecessor application, has to be uploaded. These cases are sometimes referred to as data bootstrapping. When updating software or after changes to the data model existing data have to be integrated into the new software version. This is called migration.

In case of data bootstrapping data from predecessor systems have to be adapted to the formats of the receiving system. Since quite often these data are of significant size this is usually done by program. It is therefore recommended to subject the overall data bootstrapping process to acceptance procedures as well. The same should be done for migrations. As a consequence more time between software acceptance and putting into production is required. This has to be taken into account in the planning process.

The necessary time not only refers to the technically required time to upload a dump or update a data base. Much more time is necessary to check out the data quality in the target system, after uploads have been completed. Often data records have a different structure than in the source system, or new items have been added or existing ones left out. The total quality is, however, not only measured by the number of record rejections during migration but has to be checked for content by random sampling of transferred data.

During preparation already existing data to be transferred have to be cleaned up before, relieved from "dead wood" and inconsistencies. This work should not be done later on in the target system.

Of course, as with everything else data bootstrapping or migration is mostly done under time pressure. This should not discourage the project. Again: these tasks have to be done one way or another anyway. What will be neglected during the preparation phase has to be caught up later by cost intensive data clean up projects.

© Springer-Verlag Berlin Heidelberg 2014
W.W. Osterhage, *IT Quality Management*, DOI 10.1007/978-3-662-43767-4_6

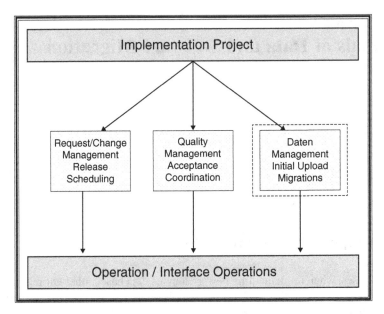

Fig. 6.1 Sub-project data migration/initial upload

It is obvious that data bootstrapping and migration are sub-projects in their own right within the overall project organisation. Figure 6.1 shows a possible structure.

6.2 Migration Systematics

The migration systematics can be seen from Fig. 6.2.

The task can vary in complexity and effort. When changing the data model additional aspects come into play as compared to a simple functional change within a release. This means that a comprehensive concept for migration has to be drawn up and documented as a kind of functional specification. This concept has to be agreed upon by all parties concerned:

- Business units
- IT
- Overall project management
- Sub-project "Migration".

The document is based on the following gross structure:

- Functional and technical background of the migration
- Initial data base in structure and content
- Target data base in structure and content
- Sequence of technical migration steps including fall back scenarios.

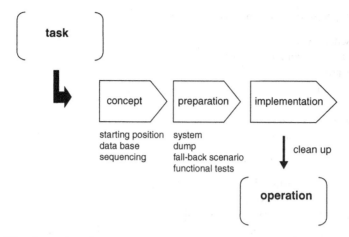

Fig. 6.2 Migration systematics

For each migration module the responsibilities for communication and partici-pating systems have to be defined. Mutual understanding of responsibilities is important—just as with any acceptance process in general. Again in this case as well everything should be arranged early on in a dedicated kick-off. During the kick-off the "internal sponsor" should be identified. Contrary to the clear terms accompanying the delivery of a release by an external supplier the initiative for migration comes from within the company itself. It is quite often addressed to a service provider residing in the same company. These relationships and responsi-bilities have to be worked out explicitly—best by service level agreements.

Another important part of the functional specifications is a check list which not only documents the time sequence of the migration steps but also all preparation measures making the process possible in the first place.

Contrary to pure functions the content to be accepted has to be defined separately. This touches upon questions concerning data consistency, tolerances and data volume including quality and quantity. An appropriate data controlling has to be set up.

6.3   Planning and Implementation

A careful preparation will later save cost intensive repetitions and data clean-up measures. The target system has to deal with twice the data volume. It has to be decided whether a test run on a separate test system using a representative selection of data should be executed to begin with (to be recommended!). Prior to migration a dump of the exiting data base has to be done to be able to reconstitute the previous state under controlled conditions.

Planning comprises the following elements:

- Time schedule,
- Resources: personnel and hardware,
- Organisational structure,
- Migration procedure,
- Documentation,
- Acceptance,
- Putting into operation.

Special emphasis is to be placed on the following details:

- Assignments of responsibilities (business units/IT/project),
- Clear description of tasks,
- Clear description of the migration objects,
- Risks concerning external impact regarding possible data problems,
- Assurance of the availability of team members,
- Budget,
- Definition of acceptance criteria.

Prior to the first data upload the following pre-conditions have to be met:

- Drafting of functional specifications,
- Identification of the exiting data base,
- Clean up of the exiting data base with regard to inconsistencies, erroneous data and redundancies,
- Logical match between old and new data structures,
- Technical specification for the adjustment program,
- Specification for the system configuration for the data bootstrap,
- Definition of fall back scenario,
- Initial data controlling,
- Timely request for additional data, for example for customising,
- Provisioning of test system,
- Customising of migration system,
- Provisioning of data bootstrap interface,
- Test of data bootstrap interface.

After data bootstrap the result has to be validated. This comprises an intensive quality check of the uploaded data. This check has to be executed under the responsibility of the sub-project with the assistance of competent members of the business units concerned if necessary.

A gross plausibility check is delivered by the rejection rate of the data to be loaded. If the rate is under a pre-defined threshold the data bootstrap is regarded as successful. Subsequently two more types of checks should be carried out:

- Random sampling of the new data base with regard to correctness,
- Analysis of the rejected data records for possible reasons.

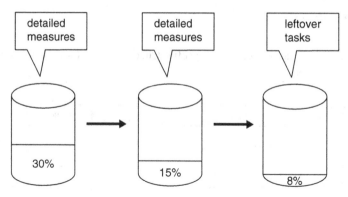

Fig. 6.3 Data clean-up

Depending on the detailed analyses manual corrections or error amendments of the bootstrap code with successive repetitions of the data bootstrap should take place. In many cases manual maintenance of the uploaded data is required when for example additional data items have been included which were not present in the old system.

For migration similar criteria as for data bootstrapping and the validation process have to be applied. Here again later data clean-up can not be excluded. It may even be in the nature of the task at hand that major data clean-up has to be carried out in any case if the coded migration algorithm is not capable to produce a clean data mapping in the first place. In such cases after migration (and this is also the case for data bootstraps as well) a sub-project "Data Clean-up" has to be set up, which takes care of the erroneous data records in the new system according to defined quality criteria. Unfortunately this may have to happen during regularly running production. Clean-up progress is depicted in Fig. 6.3.

6.4   Task Tracking

The simplest way is to record all necessary tasks in a task list (EXCEL©) (template see Sect. 6.5).

To follow up on the status three categories are sufficient:

- Open,
- Work in progress,
- Closed.

In addition finished tasks can be marked by crossing them out to have a better overview.

Another essential tool is budget tracking. Its format has been introduced already in Chap. 2.

Special emphasis has to be placed on customising a suitable test system. This will be dealt with in Chap. 7.

6.5   Templates

The following templates have proven useful: Checklist (Fig. 6.4), Data Controlling (Fig. 6.5) and Task List (Fig. 6.6).

Main Tasks	Status
define schedule	
identify source system	
initiate project	
define migration process	
define responsibilities	
estimate risks	
budget	
define acceptance criteria	
provide target system	
acceptance tests	
ensure data quality	
operation	

Fig. 6.4   Check list

source file1	target file1	nb. rejections	rejection reason	clean up measures	progress %	Status	deadline	responsible
source file 2	target file 2							
....								
source file N	target file M							

Fig. 6.5   Data controlling

Task	Date	Responsible	Status
migration planning			
write functional specifications			
identify existing data			
clean up existing data			
compare data structures			
technical specifications for migration program			
define system environment			
fall-back scenario			
initiate data controlling			
carry out customizing			
provide test system			
test of migration interfaces			
carry out migration			
draw samples			
data analysis			

Fig. 6.6 Task list

6.6 Approach

Objective: data quality and consistency > planning of migration as a sub-project: responsibilities and tasks > implementation and tracking > data quality assurance.

Chapter 7
Special Cases

The special cases to be discussed now may be treated individually or be part of the general acceptance procedures within a project where they play an important role. For these reasons some redundancies with passages from sections already presented may appear in the following.

7.1 Acceptance of Interfaces

7.1.1 Special Case Interfaces

Acceptance of interfaces may deviate somewhat with respect to the acceptance procedures already discussed because they may demand higher attention. The main reasons for this are:

- Participation of business units already during the development phase and/or
- The provisioning of special data.

7.1.2 Completeness of the Test Environment

Acceptance of interfaces either outside or in connection with the delivery of a new release presents a particular challenge to acceptance procedures for the following reasons:

- Preparation of interface files in the correct format for export or import with a sufficient number of data records to permit bulk tests,
- Availability of test environments of partner systems,
- Link up to partner systems,

© Springer-Verlag Berlin Heidelberg 2014
W.W. Osterhage, *IT Quality Management*, DOI 10.1007/978-3-662-43767-4_7

- Availability of test personnel for the partner systems,
- Creation of log files for the evaluation of interface runs,
- Alternatively: creation of synthetic data records.

7.1.3   Dedicated Procedure

The increased complexity generated by these additional requirements has to be met by dedicated procedures. In particular they comprise the following measures:

- Simulation of interface runs,
- Early involvement during the development phase,
- Evaluation of test protocols from the development phase,
- Combination of synthetic and real production data for acceptance tests,
- Integration of these elements into the standard acceptance process.

7.1.4   Simulations and Multi-stage Procedure

7.1.4.1   Simulation

A realistic interface test demands the link up of two or more partner systems. The logical addressing of the systems has to be known and mutual access rights have to be released. Thereafter the appropriate data packets have to be generated on the exporting system and the interfaces triggered to permit the transfer. After this the import into the opposite system has to be checked and validated against the export.

Because of frequent technical (parallel availability of all system components) and political (system sovereignty) restrictions the above described procedure may be shortened to gain plausible results in spite of these constraints. To achieve this, interface simulations can be employed.

This means that on the same host system an export file has to be generated synthetically possessing the expected transmission format. For this certain pre-conditions have to be respected:

- The file has to be sufficiently large to permit performance tests. For this reason in most cases a purely manual creation of data records is not sufficient, and a data record generating program has to be written. This will produce additional costs.
- Common errors have to be built into the file as they are expected to happen in real business scenarios. These errors serve to provoke interface rejections.
- This artificial test file is now transferred via an interface run of the import part to the system under acceptance tests and the results analysed later.
- Vice versa a generated export to a partner system can be copied into a local file and then compared with the expected results.

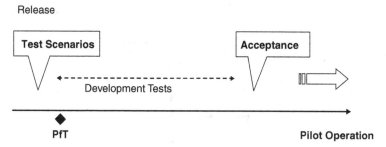

Fig. 7.1 PfT interface testing

7.1.4.2   Integration into Test Phase

As already mentioned the acceptance test phase by the customer is preceded by
testing during development. During this earlier phase the developers themselves
carry out tests. In the course of quality assurance in the development team these
tests are documented in scripts.

To gain time in the acceptance test phase itself it has proven useful to let
representatives of the customer participate in these tests even before an interface
is officially provided for acceptance proper. This procedure is depicted in Fig. 7.1.

7.1.4.3   Interface Acceptance: Time Schedule

PfT is the date of provisioning for tests. These tests are—as already mentioned—
internal tests. Before the official start of acceptance procedures the customer may
accompany these internal tests. This is a question of negotiation with the software
supplier. Since a timely implementation is generally of interest for both parties the
supplier normally is quite willing to let this happen.

Once the interface tests during development come to a positive result acceptance
may be granted under the condition of pilot operation. This makes sense since test
conditions during the development phase are different from formal customer
acceptance procedures. To be on the safe side a time window has to be defined
for this pilot operation under production conditions after putting the system into
service. During this time the usual warranty conditions of the supplier still have
validity (cost free amendments of possible errors popping up).

Step by Step Process

Altogether two scenarios can be envisaged which deliver the results so far discussed
in practise:

Step 1

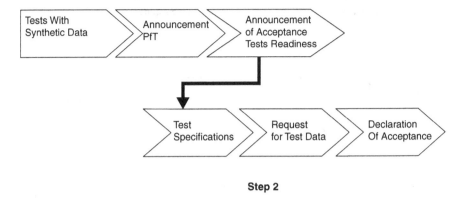

Step 2

Fig. 7.2 Two-step-approach

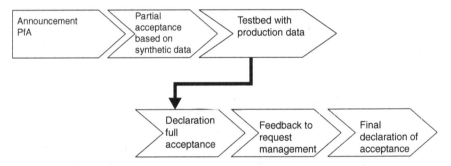

Fig. 7.3 Special interface acceptance procedures

1. Interface acceptance in phase with other software acceptance (for example releases) and
2. Interface acceptance as a separate action.

Figure 7.2 depicts the first case.

Step 1: The supplier carries out his tests with synthetic data in accordance to the technical and his own test specifications. Once a quality assured state is reached provisioning for test is declared to the customer who in turn acknowledges acceptance readiness.

Step 2: The customer gets access to the test specifications of the developers and requests the necessary test data for his purposes. After successful verification acceptance is declared.

Figure 7.3 describes this special case.

The supplier tests as described above with synthetic data in accordance to the cleared technical specifications. Just as for normal acceptance procedures he declares the provisioning for acceptance. In a first step acceptance tests are executed with synthetic data by the customer. Because of the high effort usually demanded only after successful tests with synthetic data a test bed with real production data is built. In case of positive results acceptance is declared by the customer after applying both procedures (synthetic and real). In this case errors resulting from the data sources used are irrelevant for the final evaluation. After this request management receives a feedback and acceptance is declared formally.

Log File Analysis

There are a number of instruments to analyse the results of interface tests including:

- Functional results,
- Comparison between export and import,
- Analysis of log files.

The matching of a functional result—for example the execution of a plausibility check—is carried out in analogy to the acceptance tests of any normal function and will not be discussed here any further.

The instruments "comparison export and import" and "analysis of log files" have to be viewed together. The comparison of data having been exported from one system and imported into another one refers to the total number of data records in question as well as to the quality of the import itself regarding the correctness of the transfer. If errors occur the analysis of the corresponding log files can be of great help. For this purpose logging has to be triggered for the test.

Log files can be kept in different formats. For this reason it is important to demand a readable format from the developers into which the required information has to be written. The format should also allow processing its contents (compress, select etc.) with existing evaluation tools. Such tools could be EXCEL © tables or for example ACCESS © data bases. The information to be registered concerns all transactions occurring during the interface operation. But they in turn can be reduced to the relevant ones by clever filtering.

If rejections occur at the interface—meaning that the number of import records is not identical to the number of export records—log files will provide information about the reasons for rejections since the corresponding entries will normally contain error comments by the system. In this way this information indicates the direction into which to search for the deeper causes.

7.1.5 Approach

Planning interface acceptance as a separate event > integrate all participating systems > special procedures depending on the constellation > multi-step procedure > log file analysis.

7.2   Customising Test Systems

7.2.1   Simulation of Production Environment

Of course, new software updates to be put into production are written with the intention to support the business environment of the customer and then be delivered for acceptance. This means that certain customer specific parameters have to be set already during the acceptance phase. For reasons of efficiency these parameters are usually not hard wired, i.e. not fixed in the code itself, but declared as variables. Creating a meaningful test configuration means also tuning the functions to be accepted with a view on their future usage. This procedure is called customising. Customising of the acceptance environment offers another advantage in the sense that during this phase the customising itself becomes an object for acceptance testing, which means that a dump of the test environment can be used to put the system into production later.

7.2.2   Business Know How

Figure 7.4 shows in a schematic way the items to be taken care of for customising.

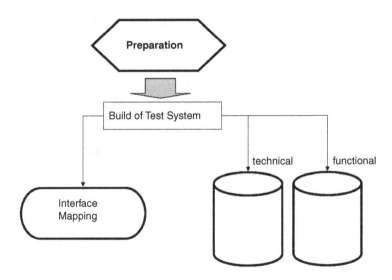

Fig. 7.4 Customising criteria

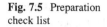
Fig. 7.5 Preparation check list

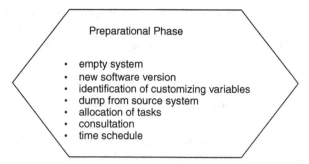

7.2.3 Separate Milestone

After a preparation phase (see below) the test system is built as an empty basic configuration without data upload. Before the first data can be loaded a customer specific structure has to be set up. The relevant customising consists of a technical and a business related part. Interfaces have to be regarded separately taking into account the partner systems to be included. Other separate subjects are the treatment of error codes as well as the layout of log files.

Before the start or during acceptance testing but not later than after the data upload customising should undergo separate acceptance tests. After acceptance the transfer to the production environment can be carried out.

7.2.3.1 Preparation Phase

In this phase representatives of computer operation, development and end users come together under the guidance of the acceptance coordination. A checklist like in Fig. 7.5 is established.

Early enough before the PfT date the main tasks will be allocated to the responsible persons with fixed target dates. Basically, the following will be decided upon:

- Sizing of the test system including all necessary access rights for acceptance testers; its logical address
- Final status of the new software version with all components required (GUI, functions, interfaces)
- Identification of customising variables
- Origin of data dump for first upload: source system (see below).

The customising variables are separated into technical and business related ones. At this point it is important that the contents of these variables are finalised. To do this, it is sometimes necessary to address different business units, for example finance for financial company codes. For this again the responsible persons for acquiring this information should be named.

It is quite possible that the overall data content has to be loaded from different source systems. In this case the exact sequence has to be established since interdependencies between individual uploads may exist.

7.2.4 Consulting Business Units

Technical and business relevant customising can be done in parallel. Sometimes technical assumptions have to be done when setting up the basic configuration. These may include for example table configurations, data buffers, configuration parameters for job streams, logical addressing, data paths etc.

Business relevant customising is very specific to the application and on top of this depends on business processes regarding the company's business and its internal organisation. One important component concerns the general rules for access rights in view of the technical possibilities at hand. This comprises among others: who has the right to read which data, change them, to execute which function etc.? This not only refers to the access rights as such but in consequence also to menu and transaction control: the end user should be offered only such functions which he needs for his job.

Other special aspects regard locking mechanisms on data items, descriptive transaction codes, number ranges, accounting keys, descriptive texts, value ranges, client structures, non standard reports and others. Since this may comprise a multitude of parameters depending on the application in question it is not possible to present a comprehensive list here.

In large corporations the business customising normally cannot be set up by one single person but has to be worked out in consent from the inputs from different business units. The effort in the preparation phase should not be underestimated.

7.2.4.1 Interfaces

Special attention regarding customising requirements is needed with respect to interfaces. Figure 7.6 shows this relationship.

Only very rarely do the data formats on both sides of an interface correspond as 1:1 for linked up systems. Often interface data records on the exporting system are composed from different table entries providing the information content. These data are then presented in an export format at the interface itself.

When importing, the corresponding system takes the information it needs and converts it in such a way as to match its own data model. Therefore a correspondence between both systems has to be created. This happens via so called mapping tables.

Mapping tables are filled with appropriate format defaults or required contents respectively for each data attribute to be transferred. In this way all export data records are generated. On the opposite side the import mapping table converts the

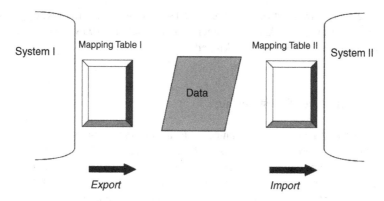

Fig. 7.6 Customising interfaces

formats handed over correspondingly. When exporting, sometimes a mapping table can be superfluous when the export interface has been written accordingly.

The contents of mapping tables can be technical or business related: for example contract codes, tariff categories, length of postal addresses etc. All this depends of course on the application and can thus not be generalised.

7.2.4.2   Error Codes

It is well known that error messages generated by the system are generally useless for the common user. For this reason most applications produce their own error messages using special routines. Regarding language as well as contents of dedicated error messages the message files are subject to specific customising.

7.2.4.3   Log Files

Log files used to record transactions need special attention regarding two aspects:

- Formatting,
- Selection.

When formatting, care has to be taken to clean the records from technical information. This means that everything related to transaction codes and data encryption, format references etc. should be left out. Only meaningful text information should be recorded giving to the evaluator a clear picture of the transaction events.

The selection of transactions to be recorded should be limited to those of primary interest for later analysis. Ancillary function calls such as "show date", "return to main menu" and others should be skipped.

7.2.4.4   Acceptance of Customising

Very similar to functional acceptance tests a correct customising can only be verified through appropriate test cases. These should be defined in consultation with and executed by the business end users. Concerning textual adjustments only, visual inspections suffice. Default menu paths have to be run through and log files triggered. More effort has to be invested when accepting mapping tables. In these cases a deeper analysis of error protocols is necessary to be able to distinguish customising errors from other interface malfunctions.

Adjustments resulting from technical customising sometimes can prove their validity only under full productive operation (configuration parameters); otherwise one has to have a completely mirrored system for bulk tests available. But again also in this case the precise addressing of destination systems can only be checked under real conditions.

Acceptance procedures for customising generally follow the same lines as usual with corresponding final documentation.

7.2.4.5   Handing Over

From the discussion above it follows that customising can be an extensive piece of work. Therefore one has to make sure to invest this effort only once. Since it has to be done in any case on the test system this will at the same time serve as a basis for the future production configuration. Procedures follow this line:

1. Build of test system (empty data base)
2. Technical customising
3. Business related customising
4. Data upload
5. Dump
6. Acceptance
7. Software amendments
8. Build of productive system (empty data base)
9. Upload dump
10. Clearance for production.

It is quite possible that certain elements of the technical customising are independent of the dump or only possible after data upload. This depends on the architecture of the application. In this respect the sequence discussed above has to be interpreted as being ideal.

7.2.5   Templates

Table 7.1 Overall checklist customising

Task	Deadline	Status
Sizing of Test System		
Latest Status Software Version		
Identification of Customising Variables		
Dump Source		
Basic Configuration		
Technical Customising		
Customising Interfaces		
Functional Customising		
Upload		
Dump		
Acceptance Customising		
Software Corrections		
Build of Productive System		
Upload Dump		
Clearance for Production		

7.2.6   Approach

Mapping of the productive environment in question > consulting business know how > mile stone planning with checklist > taking care of special cases (interfaces, error codes, log files) > acceptance > production.

7.3   Building a Test System

7.3.1   Technical Preconditions

This section deals with how to build a system (Fig. 7.7) on which a software shall be implemented which is already in use elsewhere and thus had been accepted previously.

Altogether the following elements have to be taken care of when building such a system:

• Basic configuration,
• Technical customising,
• Business related customising,

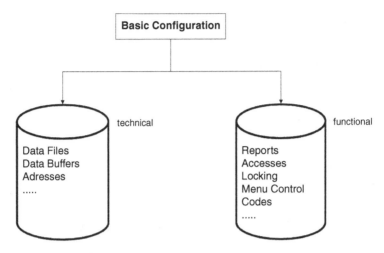

Fig. 7.7 Test system build

- Uploads (for example from previous versions of the productive system; not to be discussed further here).

7.3.2   Adequate Configuration

The basic configuration is uploaded onto an empty hardware or partition and contains the new software version to be tested (release, service pack etc.) as well as an initialised but empty data base. This environment will be provided and can then be prepared according to the specific demands of the customer.

7.3.3   A Stand Alone Milestone

The following describes the necessary steps to be observed when building a new system with existing applications. Aspects of quality assurance and relevance to acceptance play the most important roles. The presented step sequence is at the same time also the chronological sequence of the overall process. In this respect this section can be regarded as a guideline.

7.3.3.1   Functional Specifications

All requirements to build this system translated into tasks in the following should be described in functional specifications. These functional specifications not only contain the technical sequence of the procedure but also all business and company related information for the requirements in question. For preparation and clearing the usual rules from request management have to be observed.

7.3.3.2 Budget

On the basis of the functional specification a first budget can be drafted. The following expenditures have to be taken into account:

- Hardware (purchase, leasing or rent),
- Storage media (ditto),
- Software and interface adjustments,
- IT technical support,
- Customising,
- Support from business units,
- Overheads for project management,
- Documentation,
- Training,
- Acceptance.

Quite often the budget is alimented from different sources. In case the purchaser is a business unit he will bear most of the costs. The system components listed here initially refer to a test environment. The budget for the productive system has to be drafted separately. It is important that already early on in the process there is clarity about the total budget for system building to avoid delays right at the beginning because of financial bottlenecks or responsibilities.

7.3.3.3 Consulting Business Units

The importance to consult the business units concerned has been mentioned already in connection with budget questions (see above). But the cooperation of business units is equally important with respect to content. Their participations is necessary especially for

- Drafting functional specifications,
- The section of test data,
- Quality assurance of data,
- Customising,
- Acceptance,
- Process documentation,
- Training.

The cooperation of business units can be critical. For this reason binding dead lines and task planning right at the beginning of the project are required. Resources from business units have to be made available and allocated to the project from time to time. The business units heads should formally support the project and be in stand by for escalations.

7.3.3.4 Support from the Computer Centre

Besides support from developers the support from the computer operations centre is required for a smooth process. The tasks to be dealt with in consultation with operations are:

- Provisioning of an empty test system with the latest release including data base and storage capacities,
- Uploading to the empty system and successive dump,
- Triggering of the required job streams for data migration,
- Support during acceptance procedures,
- Possible provisioning of a training system,
- Putting the production system into operation.

Competent operations staff should be included into project planning from the very beginning.

7.3.3.5 Project Planning

When planning and building the test system basic rules of project management have to be observed. Since those have been discussed at various occasions this is not repeated here. Only this:

For the kick-off the agreed upon project manager has to invite all parties that may deliver some contribution to the project as such—including managers providing their personnel resources. It is important that at the end of the kick-off a binding assignment regarding

tasks–dates–persons

comes about. The schedule documented either as a check list or a mile stone plan is part of the official project documentation and serves as a yard stick for all future reviews.

7.3.4 Building the System

Besides using the classical tools of project management four additional instruments may help to implement this interdisciplinary enterprise:

Task				Responsible		Deadline	Status

Fig. 7.8 Status report

- Regular status meetings,
- Intermediate ad hoc reports,
- Keeping a list of open issues,
- Keeping a list of remaining issues.

Status Meetings

All participants have to be invited who may provide any contribution since the last status. Initially the overall task and action list with deadlines will be presented. Later only deviations from the original plan will be discussed. For each issue a status is kept with the follow-up to-dos. Figure 7.8 shows such a status report.

This report, including a list of participants, location and time as well as the agreed upon next steps, serves as a protocol about work progress.

Status Queries

It is often necessary for the project management to ask for an intermediate state of affairs between formal status reviews. For setting up a test system this is the case when steps on short notice such as data upload, customising etc. have to be carried out since certain follow-up activities are based upon these predecessors. In case of failures or delays of the predecessor tasks the complete project plan has to be adjusted accordingly. The project members involved have to be informed per email about these short term changes without the necessity of convening a special meeting.

List of Open Issues

Along with project progress the formal status reports will change to an open issue list (Fig. 7.9) which is worked through as a straight check at project meetings. During this project phase all members are well accustomed to each other and the issues in question are also well known, and therefore long elaborations can be spared.

List of Remaining Issues

At the end of the project i.e. after having the system installed, the list of open issues converts to the list of remaining issues. This list contains open issues, which may be important but not indispensible for the full functioning of the system. This means that the system has been practically accepted in the meantime (see below), but that

Open Issues			**Measures**		**Responsible**	**Deadline**

Fig. 7.9 Open issues list

these issues still await resolution. Thus the remaining issues list becomes part of the acceptance documentation. The timely resolution of the tasks still open has to continue to be tracked after the system has been put into service. Here are some possible remaining issues:

• Training,
• Data clean-up,
• Access rights etc.

7.3.4.1 Escalation

Just as with any other project at the start one or several escalation paths have to be defined in case it breaks down for a number of reasons. For test system build these paths can depend on the tasks outlined below. Accordingly there may be different addressees for escalations:

• Uncertainty about the responsibilities concerning data sourcing or data updates,
• Unforeseen change requests for example for interfaces,
• Creating system specific training documents,
• Responsibilities for customising.

Apart from the above there may be the usual reasons for escalations: passing deadlines, acceptance rejection etc.

7.3.4.2 Customising

The overall customising subject has been described above.

7.3.4.3 Interfaces

In case specific interfaces are required for system build their adjustments have to be documented in functional and technical specifications. Furthermore, the necessary lead times with respect to realisation has to be scheduled. Acceptance procedures for interfaces have been described above.

7.3.4.4   Test System

Technically an empty system will be provided initially with the agreed upon version of the operating system. For this provision the same customising rules as for a productive system have to be observed except for system addressing. For project planning the exact chronological sequence of the data upload is decisive. The following steps have to be observed:

- Decision regarding source systems, from which data will be obtained,
- Verification of the existence of the necessary upload interfaces,
- Time required for the upload,
- Quality assurance of upload,
- Additional migrations for improvement of the original data base,
- Quality assurance of migrations,
- Manual and automatic data clean-up,
- Defining responsibilities for continuing data maintenance,
- Backup of total test data base.

7.3.4.5   Process Documentation

The existing process documentation has to be tailored to the new system environment. In case there is no documentation at all it has to be written. In this case the usual levels have to be observed: overview documentation, detailed descriptions and work instructions. Here only the latter are of relevance. They serve as a basis for training documents. Work instructions describe the handling of the software on the system by the end user.

Additionally documents have to be drafted describing operations, the handling of interfaces as well as the triggering of reports. Of importance is also the description the error management process: support levels and escalation paths including contact persons and their telephone numbers. The documentation is part of the overall package to be accepted.

7.3.4.6   Access Rights

When implementing user access rights the following rules have to be observed:

- The access rights for the new test system usually do not fit the same persons (with the possible exception of administrators), whom they were assigned to on existing systems.

- The access rights for the test system are not the same as those for the productive system. Technical staff, trainers etc. will not obtain access to the productive system. Vice versa the personnel from business units having access rights to the test system are to be supplemented by additional users in the future.

7.3.4.7 Training

User training can possibly happen on the test system. This is an opportunity to let participants of basic training take part in the test process. Or else training takes place on a separate trainings system, being a complete mirror of the test system. This normally means putting the training on hold until the test system has been accepted to avoid undesired errors during training. As a consequence there would be a delay between the acceptance of the test system (see below) and putting the system into production due to intermediate training.

Training documents and work instructions for the application can be deduced from the process documentation (see above). Training data come from the overall data uploads.

7.3.4.8 Acceptance

Generally, when accepting a new test system the same rules apply as described in principle already elsewhere. Since for such systems short cuts or variants are possible the following options have to be checked in particular:

- Which are the relevant acceptance criteria?
- Does a declaration of operational readiness suffice?
- Is a pilot operation required?

These and similar questions have to be clarified during a clearance meeting where at the same time the test system should be approved for migration to the productive system.

7.3.4.9 Migration

Building the test system and data upload strategy are organised in such a way that a seamless transfer to the productive system should be possible. In this way any customising does not have to be repeated for example.

The first action after acceptance thus is the backup of the latest version of the test system: software, operating system, data base and all utilities. The whole package is then uploaded on the initially empty productive system. Thereafter data quality assurance takes place verifying the completeness and contents of the data upload with a possible evaluation or initialisation of data clean-up measures. Only after this the system can be cleared for productive usage.

7.3.4.10   Putting into Service

After successful acceptance (see above) and drafting the corresponding formal documents the system can be transferred to regular service. For this its completeness has again to be recorded. These are the most important elements:

- Release,
- Data base,
- Utilities,
- Documentation,
- Training,
- Access rights.

7.3.5   Templates

Table 7.2   Overall checklist for test system build

Task	Deadline	Status
Write and clear functional specifications		
Assure Budget		
Consult business units		
Organise system support		
Document tasks and deadlines		
Publish project structure		
Define escalation paths		
Implement customising		
Adjust interfaces		
Upload test system		
Data migration		
Document processes		
Release access rights		
Training		
Acceptance		
Take up operation		

7.3.6   Approach

Creating technical system as a basis > establish basic configuration > functional specification with mile stones, support and project planning > tracking > customising > documentation > training > migration > putting into operation.

7.4   Integrative Testing

7.4.1   Process Tests

Everything so far discussed about interface tests and simulations was done from a purely technical point of view. The question was: do interfaces function correctly, when transferring the requested number auf data records in a given format? In this way all interfaces within a system network can be tested successively. If no errors show up there is no technical reason why acceptance should not be granted. This is the common attitude of developers and software suppliers.

For the daily business based on software applications such a functioning is indeed assumed. In action the interfaces, however, are transparent to the user. His interest is a functioning process—in particular that part of a process for which he is responsible in daily business. In this sense his interest is in the factual result at the end of a process chain. And this requires an in-depth test methodology.

In practise this means that tests have to be integrative for acceptance. Test cases have to include all relevant sub-processes (including work instructions) on all systems linked up by their mutual interfaces (Fig. 7.10). Only after the complete chain has been passed with positive results, this part of a process can be regarded as accepted. Interfaces will only be looked at individually when specific problems have shown up during testing.

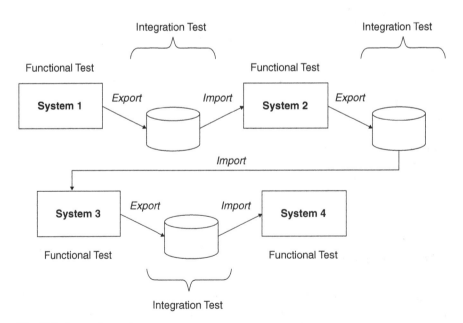

Fig. 7.10 Integrative testing

The reason for possible problems with interface performance during process tests, which have not shown up during previous individual interface tests, can be traced to the selection of acceptance criteria by the business units. Just a clean data transfer without rejections does not necessarily suffice:

- The relations between data items have to be correct.
- Plausibility checks have to function.
- Sometimes certain items have to be skipped etc.

7.4.2   Availability of Partner Systems

Integrative testing thus means the participation of all systems concerned. This means in particular:

- Availability of test systems of all participating partners,
- Willingness to participate,
- Planning together with all parties concerned,
- Collective error tracking,
- System support from all sides,
- Support by the business units.

At the same time one has to ensure that the release versions on the partner test systems correspond to those on the productive systems. To fulfil only these basic pre-conditions not only a significant planning effort is required but also political hurdles have to be overcome. In the end this boils down to making test resources available that serve the advantage of other business units. Quite often little understanding will be encountered because of tight budgets binding staff to their usual tasks. At the same time making systems technically available can be difficult since other departments may at the same time undergo system changes and tests. For these reasons it is advantageous to organise integrative tests on a higher level close to top management.

7.4.3   Integrative Testing

To fulfil the pre-conditions discussed above additional tasks have to be included in the planning surpassing acceptance procedures for individual systems. These comprise:

- Early identification of testers from all units concerned,
- Combined kick-off with the partner systems,
- Test scripts agreed upon be all parties,
- Timing of required interface runs,
- Common error tracking tool,

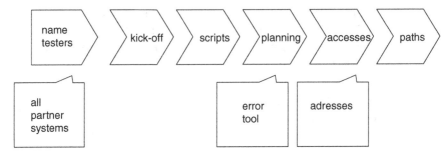

Fig. 7.11 Planning integration tests

- Release and communication of system addresses,
- Granting of the necessary access rights on alien systems,
- Provisioning of exchange directories.

Figure 7.11 shows the integrative testing systematic.

Otherwise all criteria relevant to individual acceptance or for stand alone interfaces apply correspondingly. Concerning the final acceptance document all responsible persons of the partner systems should sign it.

7.4.4   Integrative Test Scripts

An important pre-condition already mentioned is the drafting of integrative test scripts. Generally these will be developed by testers of the key system involved and consulted upon with the partner systems. Figure 7.12 shows such a test script schematically.

It is important when applying such a test script that the sequence be kept so that the necessary resources (testers and systems) can be provided at the right moment. However, there are limits to exact scheduling. If problems occur during the test sequence in a particular system or interface, unplanned delays will be the result. Reasons can be manifold:

- Configuration errors,
- Customising problems,
- Interface errors,
- Software error in system A,
- Software error in system B.

Sometimes even simple communication problems between participants suffice to bring the sequence to a halt. Delays and problem solutions are the consequence. In any case a delay means re-scheduling in the short term with all the difficulties to keep resources at the ready.

The objective of integrative acceptance is not the acceptance of a system but the acceptance of a complete process. For this reasons it is important that the signatures

No.	System	Description of Test Case	Variant	Result
1	System1	functional test 1	x1	
2	System1 System2	functional test 2, export, import, functional test 3	x1	
3	System2	functional test 4	x1	

Fig. 7.12 Integrative test scripts

of all participants from the business units concerned should appear on the acceptance protocol.

7.4.5 *Templates*

Table 7.3 Integrative test script

		System
Sub-Process Level 1		
Sub-Process Level 2		
Work Instruction		
ID		
Variant		
Input		
Output		
Acceptance Criterion		

7.4.6 *Approach*

Identification of the relevant process chain > organisational integration of all partner systems > clarification of the necessary boundary conditions > overall planning of the integration test > creating and applying integrative test scripts.

7.5   Performance

7.5.1   *Performance as an Acceptance Criterion*

When performance becomes an object of acceptance this may cause some difficulties. On the one hand there is really no special test script in the usual sense for testing. On the other hand performance itself can be extremely critical for sequences of process steps viewed by the business end user with respect to the standard he sets. When the execution of certain functions takes an unacceptably long time the business itself will be seriously impaired if not made impossible altogether. For these reasons performance can become an acceptance criterion of its own. In this context it should be regarded just as any other ordinary test case for the final acceptance evaluation of the software to be implemented.

7.5.2   *Benchmarks*

The real problem, however, is not the acceptance criterion itself but the yardstick to be employed. The subjective notion of a user sitting in front of a silent screen and waiting for the return of the cursor—the pure response time aspect—is not sufficient in most cases to represent a measurable quantity. For this reason normally no online functions or GUIs will serve for test cases but rather the duration of batch jobs, which can be quantified. The determination of CPU time or elapsed time is not difficult since these are recorded by the system itself. The difficulty, however, lies in their interpretation.

Ideally the test system represents not only the complete production configuration but also simulates all concurrent processes normally running on the production machine—including the corresponding user load during day and night time. But such a constellation is often hard to achieve with regard to costs. Furthermore doubts may continue once load distribution becomes a subject of discussion.

For these reasons one usually contends oneself with building a configuration in the following way:

* Representative data volume as a basis for extrapolation,
* Power dimensioning of the system regarding central processor and memory permitting scalability.

The measured times will be extrapolated via an agreed upon algorithm after the test runs.

7.5.3 Performance Measurements

Once criteria and algorithms have been defined performance runs should be scheduled during acceptance tests. This may happen in parallel with the usual test scenarios or during special time windows reserved for this purpose. Some times the test of a batch function can be used for performance analysis at the same time it is tested against possible errors.

7.5.4 Monitoring

Dynamic data are obtained under load as a function of time—generally under real or simulated production conditions. Other possible configurations include:

- Benchmark configurations
- An almost empty machine to test specific processes with the aim for later calibrations and scaling.

To capture dynamical performance data the market or suppliers of operating systems offer special monitors, which collect these data and visualise them on screen or make them available in file reports. Depending on the problem under consideration and on the application environment such monitors will run hours, days or even weeks either during production or in a simulation environment by using specifically developed test cases. The most important information to be collected is the following:

- Application programs currently in use,
- Distribution of user frequency over a lengthy period of time,
- Account statistics,
- Processor load,
- Main memory usage,
- Memory management,
- Number of running processes,
- Frequency of file accesses (open table),
- Overheads and interrupts,
- Waiting queues,
- System table usage,
- I/Os,
- Swap rate.

These data can be obtained either as snap shots of specific performance situations or as a dynamic collection over longer time intervals. Monitors can be supplemented by log files for system events against the backdrop of the production schedule. Furthermore there are monitors, which register system interrupts and their internal transaction times along with addresses in main memory. This detailed

information has to be brought into relation to the corresponding log files manually
for deeper analysis later. Additional tools provide for:

- Selection of main memory segments,
- Selection of specific users,
- Task related CPU time,
- Momentary execution status of programs or
- Access to selected files.

Some tools deliver process state overviews. These can comprise:

- User related information,
- % of actual CPU,
- % of actual memory,
- Actual external storage media occupancy,
- Process status (active, idle . . ..).

Time dependent data should be stored. Additionally to the monitor data the usual
system queries should be recorded:

- Current sessions,
- Jobs,
- I/Os,
- Corresponding system logs.

There is a gray area between dynamical and static data with respect to:

- The frequency of standard function calls by users and
- The production schedule.

In addition to the already mentioned reports and dynamical system information
performance monitors deliver excerpts of the impact of applications currently
running:

- Average processor usage,
- Time dependent processor usage,
- Average memory usage,
- Time depending memory usage,
- Current processes with status,
- Files opened,
- Disc occupancy,
- Communication traffic.

Figures 7.13, 7.14, 7.15, 7.16 show typical screen reports of performance
measurements (from the TuneUp © tool of TuneUp company).

Besides this general monitoring some aspects need special attention. One of
them concerns paging activity in main memory. Paging or swapping always leads to
delays in response times and thus strains the CPU as well. And then paging causes
also I/Os to the detriment of other user demands. Altogether, the fact that online

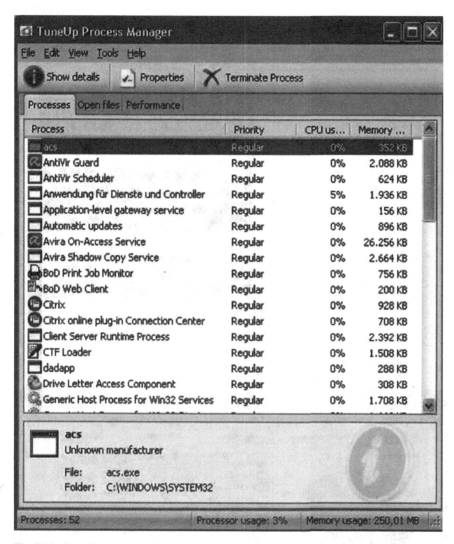

Fig. 7.13 Overall processor performance

applications normally cause more load then pure batch applications has to be born in mind, when interpreting the measured data later.

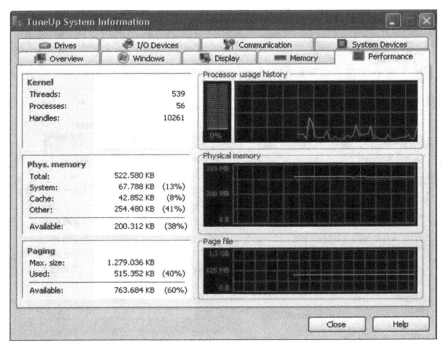

Fig. 7.14 Detailed processor load

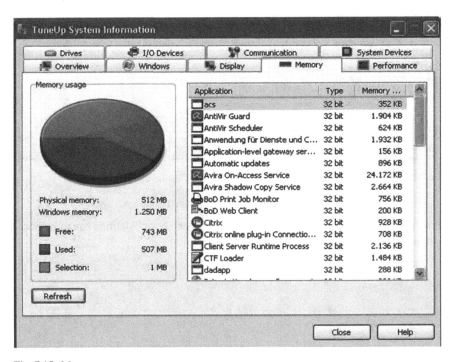

Fig. 7.15 Memory usage

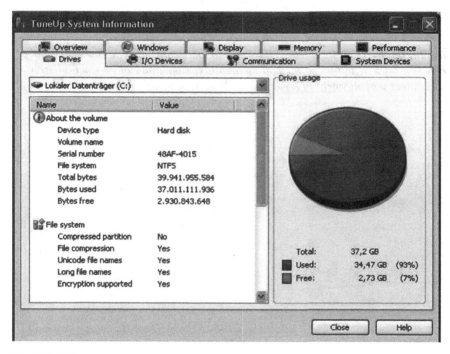

Fig. 7.16   Drive usage

7.5.5   Templates

Table 7.4   Checklist performance optimisation

Task	Done
Identification of a visible performance problem	
Recording system configuration	
Recording applications	
Recording data base management systems	
Recording production schedule	
Recording user environment	
Detailed investigation of system parameters	
Selection and installation of a suitable monitor	
Performance measurement processor, memory, communications	
Identification of spikes	
Detect average values	
Data analysis	
Identification of bottlenecks	
Draft catalogue of measures	
Implementation (short, medium, long term)	
Regression analysis after implementation	
Fine tuning measures	
Regular observations	

7.5.6   *Approach*

Identification of performance relevance to particular functions > definition of benchmarks > definition of method (scalability, simulation of production etc.) > scheduling > deployment of a monitor > analysis of measured results.

(

Chapter 8
Documentation

8.1 Types of Documents

One has to differentiate between documents being created and required before, during and after a project. These include so-called reference documents. They are necessary before and during an acceptance process to establish an unequivocal understanding of acceptance between customer and supplier. They are a mixture of technical and commercial documents which are referenced in part by the contract as the basis for implementation. Table 8.1 shows some example entries (see explanations of the field items).

Meaning of the field items:

- No.: sequential number
- File name: incl. path
- Author: responsible editor (not the user having saved the latest version)
- Document title: title in long text, for example:

  - Acceptance guideline
  - Technical specification . . ..
  - Test script for . . ..
  - Functional specification . . ..
  - Test schedule . . .. etc.

- Version: no. of released version (versioning according to ISO standard)
- Date: date of document release.

Besides these there are documents which are created during the acceptance process containing results. Here are some examples:

- Protocol of provisioning
- Problem repository
- Acceptance protocol . . ..

© Springer-Verlag Berlin Heidelberg 2014
W.W. Osterhage, *IT Quality Management*, DOI 10.1007/978-3-662-43767-4_8

Table 8.1 Reference documents	No.	File name	Author	Title	Version	Date

And finally there is the complete set of system documentation. The documentation to be delivered together with the software is described in detail in the implementation contract. It can be provided on different media:

- Paper (rather rarely),
- Data carrier,
- Electronically with the software (online),
- Electronically per link,
- Or on more than one of those media.

Normally the documentation includes:

- Description of the overall functionality:

  - Presentation of those business processes being supported by the operation of the software,

- Production schedule:

  - Job sequence including parameters and configuration particulars required for their execution,

- List of delivered items:

  - Software components, data base system, jobs, utilities etc.

- Inventory document:

  - Only when hardware is delivered at the same time by the supplier,

- Concept of operation:

  - In addition to the production schedule: data backup strategy, logging, support etc.

- User documentation:

  - Work instructions structured according to the professional responsibilities of the user usually as online help,

- Customising documentation:

  - Functional and system defaults and defaults for certain data items.

Functional and technical documentation should have the most recent release status before acceptance.

It is important that there is consensus between all parties concerned, which documents have relevance for acceptance.

8.2 Completeness and Relevance

Some indications regarding possible sources of documents have already been given in Chap. 5.

8.2.1 Completeness

There are documents which have to be ready before the start of acceptance testing and others which can be supplied afterwards. The first type includes:

- Released functional specifications,
- Released technical specifications,
- Test scripts,
- Protocol of provisioning.

The latter comprise:

- Training documents,
- Process descriptions etc.

Of cause it is desirable that all these documents are provided before the start of acceptance testing. Sometimes this is not possible because of time constraints. Of course, those documents being created during the acceptance testing itself (problem repository, acceptance protocol etc.) cannot be delivered beforehand. The complete software documentation itself will in any case only be delivered after the provisioning of the software itself.

8.2.2 Relevance

One has to distinguish between technical and legally relevant documents. One legally relevant document which at the same time serves as a basis for the billing process is the acceptance declaration with all appendices (acceptance protocol, amendment schedule). All other documents comprise technical details permitting acceptance testing in the first place and later operation. Its importance, however, lies in the fact that the total system documentation is subject to its own proper acceptance process. More details further down.

8.3 Responsibilities

According to document type specific responsibilities will be allocated (see Table 8.2).

Table 8.2 Documents and responsibilities

Functional Specifications	Business Units
Technical Specifications	Development
Documents for Acceptance Tests	Acceptance Management
Test Scripts	Business Units
System Documentation	Supplier

Acceptance management has to make sure that these documents are provided in time and released accordingly within the usual versioning and clearance process.

8.4   Versioning and Releasing

For documents, which do not have operative relevance (such as the problem repository or the acceptance declaration), but contain basic information, a versioning process should be established. The coding systematic could be as follows:

x, y with

- x: version number and
- y: indication of release status.

The release status can be coded as follows:

- 0: draft
- 1: in consultation
- 2: released.

Additional fine tuning is possible.

During the consultation process comments and amendments from different participants will be solicited to be integrated into the follow-up versions. This total history will be kept in a table at the end of a document (Template see Sect. 8.5) such that the evolution of a document can be traced back later. It is quite possible that controversies arise about the most recent valid status when mistakes have been made during releasing and distribution. The history is a sure instrument to clarify these problems.

8.5   Templates

The following templates are useful: release history (Table 8.3), list of work supporting tables (Table 8.4):

Table 8.3 Release history

Version	Status	Date	Responsible	Comment
0.1	Intermediate			First draft
0.2	Intermediate			Update
0.3	Intermediate			Update
0.4	Intermediate			Update on the basis of comments from . . ..
1.0	Released		see above.	

Table 8.4 Set of work supporting tables

Release Histories
Release of Acceptance Directive
Budget Planning
Responsibilities
Task Lists (diverse)
Problem Repository
Ideas Repository
Protocol of Provisioning
Test Schedule
Check Lists (diverse)
Acceptance Test Tasks
Acceptance Objects
Reference Documents

Chapter 9
Security Aspects

9.1 IT Security as Part of Quality Management

9.1.1 Security Requirements

Security requirements arise on different levels:

- At the strategic level and its relation to the overall organisation,
- As tools to satisfy certain specifications and
- Through groups of people, who are responsible for those specifications.

These different dimensions will be discussed in the following. They are in turn related to specific risk estimates and possible countermeasures.

9.1.2 Risks

Risks can be categorized multi-dimensionally:

- With respect to physical objects
- With respect to potential damage
- Or as a combination of both.

Additionally risks evolve with the progress of attacks: the further an invader progresses in a system the higher will be the remaining risk. Risks, however, can never be completely eliminated.

© Springer-Verlag Berlin Heidelberg 2014

W.W. Osterhage, *IT Quality Management*, DOI 10.1007/978-3-662-43767-4_9

9.1.3 Measures

As will be explained below, one has to distinguish between two categories of measures:

- Organisational and
- Technical.

Both operate in concert and complement each other. Measures can be of a general nature, which constitute a security environment, which broadly controls security loopholes. These include directives, organisational structures and technical security installations at hardware and software level. Additionally quite a number of specific measures exist, which cover specific security risks and are relevant for specific cases. The required processes for them to work have to be implemented.

9.2   Scope

The scope of IT security is limited by two criteria:

- Organisation
- Time.

The scope concerning organisation refers to the organisational units in a company, for which the security system and its documentation are relevant. Normally all units are included. Exceptions may be outsourced units, subsidiaries or affiliated companies. In times of transition after a merger for example the possibility exists that certain departments, which may be using different IT systems, are controlled in a different fashion. These exceptions have to be documented accordingly.

Timely restrictions of the scope refer to version levels. Every document has a version number referring to the main document. The validity statement refers to the actual version, exceptionally sometimes also to sections of past versions. In any case: the latest update is relevant. This comprises statements as to how individual documents are processed. Changes are to be recorded in a version history up to the final release.

9.2.1 Normative References

The whole subject of IT security is also influence by national standards and directives, some of which will be briefly mentioned. Detailed information can be obtained from the original documents:

9.2.1.1   Legal Regulations

Every country issues laws, which may also be relevant to IT security under different aspects. These include:

- Data privacy protection
- Laws regulating information and communication services
- Laws regulating telecommunications
- Signature regulations and
- Many others.

9.2.1.2   Guidelines and Standards

Government agencies offer guidelines based on international standards concerning IT security. Three of these standards will be outline in the following:

9.2.1.3   Standard ISO/IEC 13335

This standard together with the two others to be presented here were developed in cooperation with the International Electro-technical Commission in Geneva. The document outlines general principles as a reference base for more specific standards. It mainly contains:

- Concepts and models for security in information and communication technology,
- Technical preconditions for the management of security risks and
- Guidelines concerning network security.

9.2.1.4   Standard ISO/IEC 17799

This standard offers approaches and step sequences for the strategic implementation of IT security systems. Detailed technical instructions are not included in this document. Its character is recommendatory without any binding force.

9.2.1.5   Standard 27001

The title of this standard reads: "Information Technology—Security Techniques—Information Security Management Systems Requirements Specifications". This standard also has recommendatory character. Technical instructions for implementation are not given.

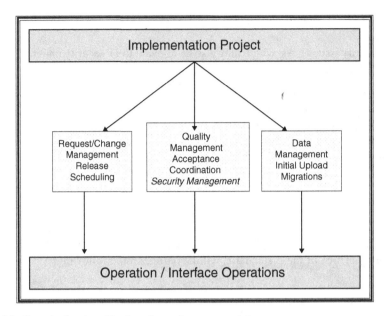

Fig. 9.1 Organisational positioning of security management

9.3   Information and Communication Security

IT security plays a major role, when systems are implemented. It can be regarded as a stand-alone subject or be part of IT quality management in general. Even if a separate IT quality organisation exists, mutual connections and interdependencies are so multiple that the one cannot be considered without the other. IT quality management is a precondition for a clean implementation of security measures. On the other hand: without consideration of security aspects there will be no sustainability in quality control.

Figure 9.1 shows the relationship between IT quality management and IT security in an overall project:

The compliance to security requirements depends on the strategic placement of these tasks in a company as a whole. It will be outlined, which preconditions have to be initiated for this role. Important is the involvement of all project stakeholders.

9.3.1   Strategic Involvement

IT security management is part of the overall security management for the whole company—all other material and immaterial goods as well as all employees. As such IT security management should be integrated methodically into the general security processes. When talking about IT security management it is understood that the whole complex of IT and communication security is meant.

IT security is achieved by a number of conceptual and organisational measures as well as by necessary technical preconditions, which are essential to reach defined security objectives. These are the areas of concern:

* IT processes
* Computer systems
* Hardware
* Software
* Communication installations
* Data and
* Documentation.

Security and Safety Engineering is the platform, on which technical preconditions for IT security can be created. The requirements can be derived from security criteria specific to a company, determined by the hierarchy after consulting with security experts. Among them are such classical criteria as

* Data integrity
* Confidentiality etc.

together with for example availability and authenticity. If a company deploys wireless communication networks, these criteria will be different from those for pure LAN applications. The main basis at the top level should be a mutually agreed and communicated security policy. Security policy should be positioned as part of the company's guiding principles, and should be furnished with the necessary competences at top management level.

On the basis of these definitions documents structured in hierarchical order are drafted on the various execution levels, transforming these guiding principles into directives to be filled with life.

9.3.2 Security Organisation

As a matter of course all employees and therefore all members of a project team have to be briefed about all valid security directives in a company. This may happen in the instant of account provisioning by transmitting this information with other account instructions. In some cases, such as WLAN operation, the person in question should receive the pertinent instructions. Instructing administrators should be obligatory in any case, since these persons have access to sensitive company and configuration data. Security requirements for administrators normally exceed those of common users.

After successful training, instruction and receiving the relevant security documentation every employee has to acknowledge by his signature on a special form that he has been informed, that he agrees with the directive and will respect it. The signed acknowledgement has to be archived by the IT security organisation.

Table 9.1 Checklist IT security

Does an IT security management exist?	IT security management deals with all security aspects concerning implementation and operation of IT installations
Have the concerns of IT security management been documented?	Pre-condition for an effective IT security management is the relevant documentation
Are current IT standards taken into account with respect to security management?	ISO/IEC 13335, 17799, 27001
Have IT security criteria been documented?	Security is classified according to such criteria as confidentiality, availability, integrity etc.
Will the participants of IT security trainings acknowledge their participation by signature?	The participation in security trainings should be documented in the interest of all parties concerned
Is the adherence to security directives monitored regularly?	The monitoring of the adherence to security directives should follow a dedicated action plan

Table 9.1 recapitulates, which are the strategic preconditions to constitute an IT security management.

9.3.3   Approval Process

Organisational procedures have to be introduced to secure the approval of different services or objects, including:

- Allocation of accounts
- Access authorisation to applications and
- Control over terminal devices.

Normally three instances are concerned with this process:

- Applicant
- Supervisor and
- Clearing officer.

The transaction has to be documented and downstream organisational units have to be informed (controlling, procurement etc.). Once the applicant leaves the organisation all authorizations become invalid and have to be withdrawn.

9.3.4   Confidentiality

Another important transaction to improve the security of an organisation is the commitment to confidentiality. Generally such a commitment is governed by the work contract so that no separate documents have to be drafted. Furthermore these regulations are still valid for the time after a person has left an organisation.

However, occasionally the need arises for additional specific confidentiality instructions. This can be the case, when a person gets into contact with highly sensitive data while working for a specific project for example. In such cases the confidentiality commitment may include restrictive information policies against units and persons internal to the organisation. Sometimes the signature under a separate paper may be necessary. And this may not only concern data. Sometimes reports about internal processes may for example facilitate inferences about methods of payment, applications etc.

9.4 Physical Security

Besides the security problems directly connected to information and communication technology itself to be discussed further on, there are the usual security aspects concerning buildings and equipment, which in most cases have to be solved physically.

9.4.1 Physical Objects

These are security relevant objects:

- The whole area of an organisation or company
- All buildings; and especially rooms that have direct communicative access to computer systems and communication installations
- Utility services
- All hardware in conjunction with information and communication, mobile or fixed and
- The adjacent neighbourhood of the company grounds, in as much as access to internal systems may be attempted wirelessly from there.

All these installations have to be secured in different ways, whenever a direct influence is possible.

9.4.2 Access

The first and most important obstacle against non authorized access is the selective authorisation of admission to installations of an organisation. This subject will not be covered in detail here, since admission control is a science in its own right. It is important that state-of-the-art technologies be used to secure all rooms, which house central hardware for application systems, by special admission mechanisms within or in addition to the already practised admission security to the premises itself.

Terminal devices, which are placed in offices, should be physically fixed and switched off, when offices are deserted.

9.4.3   Threats

As will be outlined further down possible threats are manifold and specific for the area of wireless communications and surpass classical risk scenarios. They can be classified roughly in the following manner:

- Direct access to central hardware with the intention to destroy or disrupt operations
- Spying attempts on central applications
- Spying attempts on decentralized applications
- Attempts to manipulate central and/or decentralized data
- Deployment of malware and
- Theft of terminal devices.

In addition there are many more aspects, which will not be discussed in detail here.

9.4.4   Equipment

Equipment bearing a high risk potential are among others:

- Central IT installations
- Fixed peripheral devices
- Mobile terminal devices
- External storage media and
- Communication modules (modems, ports, switches etc.)

9.4.5   Utility Services

Utility services are prone to create risks, once they

- Do not function or
- Function wrongly.

Electricity supplies belong to the first category. To prevent interruptions emergency power supplies have to be on standby. Water supplies belong to the latter category, if large quantities of water penetrate computer rooms and endanger hardware due to water pipe fracture. For both cases emergency plans have to be drawn up.

9.4.6   *Disposal of Devices*

Besides the usual legal disposal regulations special attention has to be drawn to additional aspects concerning company and IT security:

- Prior to the disposal all data stored on a device—especially administration data—have to be deleted or neutralized in such a way that even accomplished technicians will not be able to re-constitute them.
- Indications to the company like type labels and inventory labels have to be removed. In this way inferences about the original company, where they were in use, should not be possible.

9.5   Documentation

These are the most important elements to be considered for individual directives:

- Subject of the directive (hardware: laptop; software: intranet for example)
- Application procedure to obtain usage rights
- Responsibilities for usage and costs
- Limitations of usage and costs
- Interdictions
- Liability and
- Damages.

Directives are of a general nature or relevant to specific fields of technologies. They can consist of the directive proper and associated implementation rules.

9.5.1   *Processes*

Quite similar to other aspects of IT quality management, the Deming Process, so called after the famous American quality guru W. Edward Deming, plays an important role for IT security philosophy with respect to verification, compliance and evolution. Figure 9.2 shows this process schematically:

As always, the same cycle refers to:

system design > implementation > analysis > improvement

A security policy has to be drafted concerning organisation and technology. On this basis implementation takes place in consultation with all parties concerned. After a certain time of operation experience is gained resulting finally into new proposals and improvements. And the whole process starts all over again. It is important to note that the operational time phase is not the same as a common trial phase. In fact this is a continuing process with fixed review intervals. The aim is

Fig. 9.2 Deming process

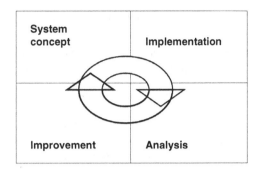

also not only to correct initial design faults. The overall process should rather make sure that—especially within the IT area—the newest technological developments are taken into account regarding security aspects.

9.5.2   Commitment

A policy or directive without commitment and the threat of sanctions only possesses its paper worth, on which it is printed. Legally there are a number of possibilities to ensure the compliance to such a document.

9.5.2.1   Noncompliance

Notice to the IT security officer.

9.5.2.2   Acknowledgement of Instructions/Sample

This directive should be part of comprehensive employee security instructions. At the end the following agreement can be signed:

Acknowledgement of the Directive

"Please read the present security directive and countersign it at the bottom of the document. One copy with your signature will be kept by the IT security officer.
With your signature you acknowledge:

- I have received the security directive, understood its meaning and agree to it.

. . ..

- <Confirmation of individual requirements from the directive>
- <Confirmation of the confidentiality clause>
- <Confirmation of liability and responsibility>

- I understand that non-compliance regarding this directive can induce legal consequences.

- Name
- Signature
- Department
- Date"

Chapter 10
Project Management

10.1 Technical and Organisational Tools

Systems supporting project management are known under the abbreviation PMS: Project Management System. We will discuss some of its features, including the following aspects will be:

- Objectives and tasks of a PMS
- Technical possibilities and functional characteristics
- The most important basic functions
- Specific functions in detail such as:

  - Task planning
  - Mile stone plan
  - Capacity management
  - Gantt diagram
  - Network diagram
  - Critical path
  - Cost control.

10.2 Objectives and Tasks

PMS is supposed to support projects above a certain complexity to ease implementation. The aim is to achieve transparency concerning:

- Project progress
- Schedule bottlenecks
- Personnel bottlenecks and
- Associated costs.

© Springer-Verlag Berlin Heidelberg 2014
W.W. Osterhage, *IT Quality Management*, DOI 10.1007/978-3-662-43767-4_10

All this is necessary to arrive in the end at the project's objectives. The effort to maintain PMS data should be in an economically reasonable relation with respect to the overall project effort. There are small projects, where one can do without expensive data capture and preparation, or where Excel© sheets cover all required demands. On the other hand, however, there are highly complex projects requiring appropriate system support. To handle these PMS applications qualified staff is needed. Depending on the degree of project complexity PMS have to be selected providing the necessary capabilities.

Besides supporting scheduling, a PMS should be capable to report about project development and disruptions, dead line transgressions, capacity bottlenecks or cost overruns. In this respects it acts as a controlling instrument.

To cover all these requirements ongoing status information about project progression itself has to be captured over and above the basic information identified to establish a project plan. By this original planning can be compared to current developments. The effort for this should not be underestimated. As for all business systems the following rule applies for PMS as well: the quality of information a system delivers depends on data quality and therefore on the input from its users. Once the decision has been taken to deploy a PMS, data maintenance should be carried out seriously. Half-heartedness leads to unnecessary effort and erroneous project documentation.

PMS generally offer a large number of possibilities to create reports for project management without having to reformat them.

10.3   PMS Functions

It would be out of proportion in this section to portray the whole spectrum of possibilities a PMS offers. Therefore the following will cover only the most important PMS functions:

- Administration of tasks
- Gantt diagram
- Mile stone plan
- Capacity management and
- Network diagram.

10.3.1   Administration of Tasks

Figure 10.1 shows a typical task list such as managed by most PMS. This list must cover all relevant individual tasks in a project. It becomes obvious already at this stage that a meaningful structuring of the overall project has to take place right from the beginning. The sequence of task processing is determined by start and end dates

Description		Total Time	Week	Day
⊟ Projects		**0:00:00**	**0:00:00**	**0:00:00**
⊟ Performance		**0:00:00**	**0:00:00**	**0:00:00**
Kick-off	▪	0:00:00	0:00:00	0:00:00
Data Capture	☐	0:00:00	0:00:00	0:00:00
Migration Preparation	☐	0:00:00	0:00:00	0:00:00
System Provision	☐	0:00:00	0:00:00	0:00:00
Migration	☐	0:00:00	0:00:00	0:00:00

Fig. 10.1 Tasks

or by task duration. It is useful to take into account the time sequence as soon as a task is entered. This will facilitate graphical presentations later.

On the left hand side we have a running number allocated by the system. The next row contains the task name in long text. This is followed by the start date. When dates are allocated the system will issue a warning when a proposed date does not exist (for example November 31st) or when it coincides with a Sunday or a public holiday. Thereafter the task duration can be entered so that the end date will be calculated. But it is also possible to define the end date, and the system then calculates the task duration. However, it is not possible to fix the duration and then trying to allocate an implausible end date.

The task can then be displayed in detail (Fig. 10.2) and supplemented with additional information.

For reasons of simplification the other rider options will not be followed through here. Basically the detailed presentation repeats the data from the task list. In addition a field showing the percentile of completion of that task appears. This field can be updated manually.

10.3.2   Gantt Diagram

The Gantt diagram shows in a well arranged fashion the most important project scheduling and progression data in one single chart (Fig. 10.3):

- The task itself along with its name
- Task duration
- Start date of the task and
- End date of the task.

At the same time a configurable calendar is displayed along the x-axis at the top. If necessary a second calendar can be shown with a different scale. In this way months can be depicted at the top und weeks on the second line or weeks above and days below. Below this calendar individual tasks are shown as time bars.

Fig. 10.2 Task detail

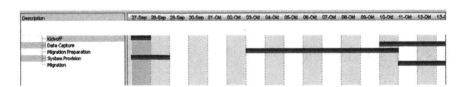

Fig. 10.3 Gantt chart

Tasks can be sorted hierarchically by grouping certain tasks together as so called collective tasks as outlined in Fig. 10.4:

The collective task "Performance" shown as a black bar comprises the individual tasks "Kick-off" and "Data Capture" and so forth. The collective task takes into account the earliest start date and the latest end date of all associated individual tasks.

At the same time the degree of completion can be displayed as in Fig. 10.5 (% completed) from the tasks processing screen.

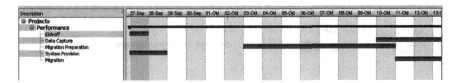

Fig. 10.4 Collective task

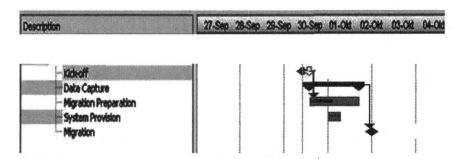

Fig. 10.5 Completion status

The degree of completion is visible as a small black bar within the task bar to document project progression. Once it has been decided to maintain this data item it obviously means extra work to be done on a regular basis.

In the presented rather simplified Gantt depictions here quite a number of refined possibilities have been left out:

- Linking of tasks
- Documentation of task owners and
- Capacity reports.

Altogether the Gantt diagram is quite possibly the most often applied chart in project management.

10.3.3 Mile Stone Plan

The mile stone plan shown in Fig. 10.6 is a kind of Gantt diagram subset.

Again all tasks can be seen and the mile stones are depicted as black rhombuses. Such a mile stone may stand at the end of a task. The task is closed once the mile stone has been reached. But a mile stone can also stand alone representing a once and for all task of very short duration—for example for a single decision to be made. Mile stones are always linked to a specific date and

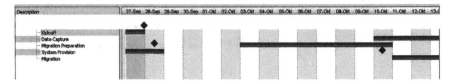

Fig. 10.6 Milestones

represent objectives or sub-goals. In this case task scheduling and its duration should be done backwards.

The system displays the date or the final date for a mile stone. This chart also shows links between predecessor and successor tasks.

10.3.4   Network Plan

Some PMS provide for network charting. Being a project control instrument a network plan displays not only chronological but also logical dependencies between tasks within a project. Depending on project complexity network plans may contain hundreds of different tasks. A grand overview of such a network plan on a wall shows impressively the total complexity of major projects in one stroke. Other conclusions that can be drawn from network plans are critical paths. Once the dependencies between tasks become transparent, consequences can be derived as to what may happen, if a critical tasks within a chain of tasks risks not to be achieved.

Chapter 11
Project Controlling

11.1 Peculiarities

IT line controlling functions basically with a view on running expenditures by organisational units. They are managed in a valid cost centre chart of accounts. Generally major investments and projects with a time limit are excluded from these procedures. For these purposes special financial resources are provided and planned separately. Thus these should be subject to their own controlling mechanisms—the IT project controlling.

The following aspects play a particular role in IT project controlling, transcending classical controlling:

- Splitting costs between different organisational units such as

  - IT
  - User departments
  - Project organisation itself
  - External support
  - Overheads (quality management, acceptance tests etc.)

- Dedicated instruments for the controlling process such as

  - Clearance procedures
  - Task confirmations
  - Project reports and other

- Differently designed controlling mechanisms: IT project controlling can advance to a project controlling instrument in its own right having influence on the overall project success.

This section will discuss these particularities in more detail.

© Springer-Verlag Berlin Heidelberg 2014
W.W. Osterhage, *IT Quality Management*, DOI 10.1007/978-3-662-43767-4_11

11.2   Objects

11.2.1   Direct IT Costs

These comprise

- Rent for server environments
- Disk drives
- Peripheral terminals
- Operations and support of test systems.

11.2.2   Costs Relevant to User Departments

These comprise:

- Drafting functional specifications
- Consulting overheads
- Training
- Test participation
- Customising.

11.2.3   Project Management

These comprise:

- Leadership and administration
- Support
- Communication and project organisation
- Reporting.

All these costs above are generated both by internal as well as external services. They have to be—as far as possible—budgeted right at project start. Furthermore a separate budget item relating to cost for outlays has to be foreseen for.

11.3   Process Approach

The process approach in this context means measures to control expenditures. In this sense they transcend a purely target-performance-comparison in reporting. They include:

- Account assignment elements
- Cost rates
- Order value procedures
- Clearance procedures.

11.3.1   Account Assignment Elements

All objects of IT controlling belonging to a specific project have to be integrated into an overall cost framework. To achieve this, a hierarchical classification as shown in the example in Fig. 11.1 is useful.

Such a structure permits a unique allocation of cost elements and at the same time a consolidation of all accumulated costs up to the highest aggregation level, which is indispensable for management.

11.3.2   Charge Rates

In addition to hourly or daily rates agreed upon by contract with external service providers there are internal charge rates in many companies between different organisational units, which have to be taken into account. If user department resources are requested, quite often such services have to be negotiated or budgeted separately. To the latter belong:

- Supporting training activities
- Participation in drafting functional specifications
- Participation in measurements etc.

PSP	3102	Upgrade Store Computer
	3102-1000	Hardware
	3102-1000-4108	Disks
	3102-2000	Software Update
	3102-2000-4322	Query Functions
	3102-2000-4323	Screen Design
	3102-3000	Process Consulting
	3102-3000-4530	Project Management
	....	

Fig. 11.1 Project cost elements accounting codes

11.3.3   Order Value Procedures

To limit budget overdraft at an early stage when buying external services, which are possibly not covered by frame contracts, most purchasing systems allow to set upper limits for the value of a single order. These restrictions can be limited to pre-defined hierarchical levels within an organisation. In this way already at the stage of invitation to bid by the initiator a warning will pop up, once a pre-defined value risks to be surpassed.

11.3.4   Clearance Procedures

The clearance of budgets or budget parts is part of a combined strategy executed in unison by requesters, project management and controlling. Most systems on the market provide professional support for such procedures. Generally the requester enters his planned demand in the system by using the available accounting structure, the project leader checks it and controlling clears it. The necessary workflows can be configured in most systems. It is important that this is preceded by prior automated checks against budget limits, charge rates and the time schedule in question before clearance proceeds manually.

11.4   Reporting

Reporting for IT projects can be quite extensive. The necessary system support is provided by many PMS (see Chap. 10) and will thus not be discussed in depth here. These are the more important reports:

- Task confirmations
- Project reports
- Budget reports.

11.4.1   Task Confirmations

A typical template for task confirmations is shown in Fig. 11.2.

Besides the time sheet itself with associated tasks the relevant accounting assignment element and possibly the order number for external partners are of prime importance to permit a unique reference to the budget.

Task Confirmation					
Project No.		**Month**		**Name**	
Date	Hours				
1					
2					
3					
4					
5					
6					
7					
8					
9					
10					
11					
12					
13					
14					
15					
16					
17					
18					
19					
20					
21					
22					
23					
24					
25					
26					
27					
28					
29					
30					
31					
Sum				**Signature**	

Fig. 11.2 Time sheet

11.4.2 Project Reports

Project reports can appear in different formats. There is no universal standard. Quite often a simple extract from the PMS does not suffice. The report should contain:

- Progress in substance
- Risks
- Adherence to schedule
- Cost development.

Only the latter is of importance here. One has to take care that the cost relevant part of the project report should be formatted in such a way that a simple transfer to the budget report is made possible. By appropriate consolidations this may lead directly to a proper management report.

11.5   Controlling

Concerning project controlling the following aspects should be taken into account. They comprise:

- Project progression and clearances
- Risks
- Advantage/disadvantage considerations.

Project progression depends of course—besides on technical requirements—on the financial resources still available. The multi-step clearance procedure serves to avoid overruns. This may lead to conflicts of interest and re-prioritisation, when several requesters have access to the same budgetary items. At this stage a clear budget structure becomes important.

Even long before a pressing clearance decision a target-performance-comparison will show the financial risks concerning project progress. It is the controllers duty to intervene anticipatory and in time and point out emerging bottlenecks. Then it is still time to organise new resources or reallocate some. Against this backdrop there exists the possibility for a reasonable evaluation of the total financial risk to a project. If warning comes too late, decisions have to be taken under duress, sometimes meaning a shortcoming of rational considerations.

Sources

This is a translation of W. Osterhage: "Abnahme komplexer Software-Systeme" (in German), Springer, Heidelberg, 2009. Parts of the book are contributions by the author to the textbook "IT Management", WEKA-Fachverlag, Kissing.

The figures referring to performance measurements in Chap. 7, Sect. 7.5, are screen shots of the performance tool "TuneUP Utilities" of TuneUP Software GmbH.

© Springer-Verlag Berlin Heidelberg 2014
W.W. Osterhage, *IT Quality Management*, DOI 10.1007/978-3-662-43767-4

Index

A
Acceptance, 1, 5, 7, 11, 40, 42, 46, 66, 74, 77, 83, 92
  procedure, 26
  protocol, 30, 101
  test, 13, 20, 21
Access rights, 40, 86, 89

B
Benchmark, 95
Budget, 42, 46, 128
Business process, 40

C
CAD, 4
Capability Maturity Model Integration (CMMI), 2
Capacity management, 120
Change management, 6, 7, 49
Change request, 10, 40
CMMI. *See* Capability Maturity Model Integration (CMMI)
Confidentiality, 111
CPU, 96
CRM, 4
Customising, 83, 102

D
Data bootstrapping, 63, 67
Data clean-up, 7, 67, 86
Deming process, 115
Directive, 41, 115, 116

Disc occupancy, 96
Dump, 80

E
ERP, 4
Error, 10–12, 18, 26, 72, 91, 92
  management, 6, 7
Escalation, 41

F
Functional specifications, 9, 21, 42, 66, 83, 103

G
Gantt diagram, 119
GUI, 94

H
Hot fix, 19
Hotline, 12, 31

I
Interface, 21, 40, 90
Inventory, 102
IT controlling, 127
ITIL, 2
IT security, 110, 111, 116

J
Job stream, 78

Printed in the United States
By Bookmasters